THE STORY OF THE AMERICAN FLAG

THE STORY
OF THE
AMERICAN FLAG

ILLUSTRATED

WAYNE WHIPPLE

APPLEWOOD BOOKS
Bedford, Massachusetts

The Story of the American Flag was originally published in Philadelphia in 1910 by Henry Altemus Company.

Thank you for purchasing an Applewood Book.
Applewood reprints America's lively classics —books
from the past that are still of interest to modern readers.
For a free copy of our current catalog, please write to
Applewood Books, P.O. Box 365, Bedford, MA 01730.

Library of Congress Catalog Card Number: 00-105700

ISBN 1-55709-501-9

10 9 8 7 6 5 4 3 2 1

THE STORY OF THE AMERICAN FLAG

The Story of the American Flag

WHAT OUR BANNER SAYS

WHEN you see the Stars and Stripes anywhere the first thing it says to you is
"Ours is a free country!"
As it waves in the breeze, it seems to be "fluttering with joy, the happiest of the happy," and to repeat, over and over,
"My country is free! This is the land of the free!—free!—free!"
Its colors—the Red, White, and Blue—sing a beautiful song together.

> Red sings: *"Be brave!—brave!—brave!"*
> White says: *"Be pure!—be clean!—be pure!"*
> And Blue sings: *"Be true!—true!—true-blue!"*

But that is not all our red, white and blue Flag tells. Not by any means. Each red or white stripe has its own history; and every white star, in its field of blue, shines with its own special glory.

The more you know about the Star Spangled Banner the better and happier you will be—and glad that you are living in the greatest and best and freest country on earth—the United States of America.

The history of the American Flag is a sad story, too—of desperate hardships, struggles and sufferings; of terrible battles on land and sea. It has gone through all these just so it may wave, as it does now—
"O'er the land of the free, and the home of the brave."

Still the Story of the American Flag is as entertaining as any romance, and as thrilling as any tale of adventure you ever read or heard. And every stripe and star, yes, every red, white, or blue thread of our dear old Flag is woven with history—the history of the United States.

9

GESSLER'S HAT USED AS A FLAG

THE FIRST FLAGS THAT EVER WAVED

DID you ever go out to have a good time by trolley, train or boat, and, when you saw another company of young people, wave your hat or handkerchief at them? And didn't they wave back at you? In waving at one another, each party seemed to say to the other:

"How do you do? We are having a jolly time and we hope you are, too!" And how heartily you all laughed!

In this way a girl makes a flag of her handkerchief, and a boy makes a kind of banner of his cap. Did you ever hear the story of William Tell? Gessler the Austrian tyrant hung his own hat up on a pole and tried to make all the Swiss men cheer it. But William Tell would not, and they took him to prison. When Gessler heard that Tell was such a sure shot with the cross-bow, the tyrant made Tell shoot an apple off his son Albert's head, as the price of his liberty. Cruel Gessler hoped Tell would shoot his boy, or, perhaps, put his eye out. But Tell did nothing of the kind. He split the apple right in two with his first arrow. Just then another arrow dropped from the inside of Tell's coat. Gessler asked what that arrow was for; Tell answered:

"For your heart if I had hurt my boy!"

Then Gessler the tyrant would not let William Tell go free. But after a long, long while he managed to escape to his home in the beautiful mountains of Switzerland.

Gessler's hat, on a pole, was the flag of a tyrant for men to bow down before. But the cap was sometimes used by the ancients, and by the French in Napoleon's day, as a banner of freedom, and called "the liberty cap."

The oldest flag, not the woven flag itself but the oldest *kind* of a flag, in the world that is still the same design that waved thousands of years ago is the simple flag of Japan, like a great white handkerchief with a round red spot in the center. This came to be made larger and larger, and to be mounted on a spear, then on a staff, then on a pole. The Chinese may have had a flag before this kind of Japanese flag was made, but Chinese flags have changed in pattern or design while the Japanese banner has always remained the same white sky with a red sun in the center.

THE FLAG OF JAPAN

The simple white and red flag looks as lovely to the boys and girls of old Japan as our beautiful red, white and blue Stars and Stripes to us.

THE FIRST FLAG THAT WAVED OVER AMERICA

A S this is the Story of the American Flag we cannot say much about the banners of other nations, interesting as that would be, excepting only the flags that have something to do with the making of ours, or with our country itself.

When Columbus landed on Cat Island, in discovering America, early on Friday morning, the 12th of October, 1492, the first thing he did was to set up a staff with a flag on it, to take possession of the newly found country in the name of the king and queen of Spain.

Ferdinand and Isabella were the rulers of the countries of Castile and Leon (or Castle and Lion as we would say), the two smaller kingdoms that made up the most of Spain at that time. So the flag that Columbus planted in the newly discovered country had two castles and two lions on it.

THE FLAG OF CASTILE
AND LEON

Poor Columbus had gone wandering about from country to country trying to raise money enough to hire ships and men to make a voyage around the world. He believed the world to be round, and felt sure he could go around it by going west instead of east.

So when he found this new land he took possession of it in the name of the king and queen of Spain. He thought he had reached India, though he was not half way there. This is why he called the red skinned natives he found *Indians*.

When the other rulers in Europe heard of the great country that had been discovered by "sailing out into the West," they all sent their bravest captains and sailors to see what they could find, and to take possession of all the land they could get at in the names of their own kings and queens.

Italy sent Americus Vespucius, England sent John and Sebastian Cabot, the Dutch sent Hendrik Hudson, France sent Jacques Cartier, and so on. Italy did not gain any land, but its man, Americus, managed somehow to give his name to the whole of the New World, as it has always been called. The new-found continent should have been called Columbia, in honor of Columbus.

The Landing of Columbus

CORTEZ'S FLEET SAILING FOR MEXICO

THE COLONIES IN AMERICA AND THEIR HOME FLAGS

THE oldest real flag in America, and doubtless the oldest actual banner in the world, is that which was carried by Cortez, the Spanish general, soon after the discovery of America, while conquering Mexico. Cortez found the Aztecs, who lived there, highly civilized, and governed by the great Emperor Montezuma, who reigned in that wonderful city built on an island in the center of a beautiful lake, now called the City of Mexico. But there was a little country in Mexico, about as large as a county in one of our States, in which the Tlascalans lived and elected their rulers as we do now. Tlascala was then a little old Republic, when all the nations in the world, New and Old, were governed by kings and queens.

Of course, the other Aztecs, and Montezuma, their Emperor, thought the Tlascalans were all wrong, and the poor little Aztec Republic had a pretty hard time of it, fighting with their neighbors and Montezuma's soldiers for their rights. So, when the strange white men came from the East and promised to help them against the Emperor and to let them vote for their rulers ever after, they were glad to help Cortez and his conquering band.   They knew the Aztec customs, acted as interpreters, and greatly aided the Spaniards in the conquest of Mexico.

As a reward Cortez gave his faithful allies the splendid flag he carried.   It was ten feet long and forked at the end.   On it was painted a beautiful figure of the Virgin wearing a crown of gold.   The Tlascalans kept the flag, but when the Spaniards got control of the whole

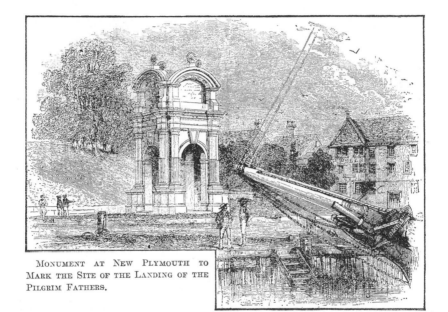

MONUMENT AT NEW PLYMOUTH TO MARK THE SITE OF THE LANDING OF THE PILGRIM FATHERS.

country they forgot their promises to their faithful allies—for Spain was governed by a king and had no use for a Republic after all.   So the poor Tlascalans were treated cruelly and shamefully.   They were enslaved by the Spaniards and compelled to work in the Mexican gold mines.   But the beautiful flag was preserved and is still kept in the National Museum of the City of Mexico.

The Lion-and-Castle flag of Spain floated over Florida for many years, where the Spanish city of St. Augustine is the oldest city in the United States, even older than the old Spanish town Santa Fé, New Mexico. There was a period, about one hundred years after the discovery of America, when there were no settlements of white people in

America, and it began to look as though Columbus's voyages had been made in vain.

But, early in the seventeenth century, ships began to arrive, flying the flags of England, the Netherlands, France and Sweden. Each shipload of men and women made settlements in Virginia, New Netherlands, New England and New France. Virginia and New England are the only colonial names that have been preserved to the present day.

ONE OF RALEIGH'S SHIPS

Captain John Smith came flying the king's colors, with the cross of St. George, up the river of Virginia which he called James, in honor of King James of England, and founded Jamestown, named for the same king. This was in 1607. Two years later Hendrik, or Henry Hudson sailed into the mouth of the river which still bears his name, in his good ship, the *Half Moon*, flying the Dutch colors, and began the settlement of New Amsterdam.

The *Mayflower*, bringing the Pilgrim Fathers and Mothers to land on Plymouth Rock, had the white flag of England, with the red cross of St. George, at the top of its foremast.

The several settlements from Europe soon grew and spread into as many colonies, loyally flying the flags of their mother countries. If England had always been kind and tender toward her American colonies they would not have left her.

THE MAYFLOWER AT NEW PLYMOUTH

PURITANS BEFORE KING JAMES   17

But she neglected her children across the seas, and afterwards treated them more like an unkind stepmother than an "own" mother.

THE CROSS OF ST. GEORGE

After the American people were greatly aroused the King of England and his ministers tried to avert the War of the Revolution by offering to grant the angry colonists many of the rights they claimed, but it was too late. "The war had actually begun."

PATRIOTS PREPARING FOR WAR

THE DUTCH SURRENDER TO THE ENGLISH

HOW THE CROSS OF ST. GEORGE WAVED OVER ALL THE OTHER FLAGS

THE English, Dutch and Swedish settlements grew to be communities, then extended till they were called colonies, then provinces. The Plymouth colony spread out till it touched the Massachusetts Bay colony on one side and the Connecticut and Providence colonies on the other. The Boston and Salem settlements were soon included in one and the same colony.

At the same time the English and the Dutch struggled for the possession of New York, as the English called it, or New Amsterdam, as the Dutch had named it. The English won the fight, and the cross

2—*The Story of the American Flag.*

of St. George waved over New York for a few years. Then the Dutch beat the English and the flag of the Netherlands floated over the same city; then it bore its Dutch name. The English finally conquered the Dutch in New York, and the Swedes in New Jersey.

Meanwhile, William Penn, the great Quaker, came from England, in

BUILDING HOUSES AT PLYMOUTH

1682, in the ship *Welcome,* flying the English flag, and settled in the country south of New York and west of New Jersey, on land which he purchased from the Indians and named Pennsylvania, a Latin name meaning "Penn's woods." He also founded the city of Philadelphia, the name being made of two Greek words, which mean "Brotherly Love."

So, you see the English conquered and crowded out the people from other countries, excepting the French in the north and northwest, and the Spaniards in the south and southwest.

In the meantime the American English men and women and boys and girls were true and loyal to their Mother Country, England. They got their best clothes, furniture and farming implements—even many good things to eat and drink from there. Parents who were able to do so sent their children to English schools and colleges. They always spoke of England as "Home." The king of England was their king and the English flag was their flag.

There was trouble over the English flag when Governor Endicott, of the Massachusetts Bay colony, cut the red cross out of the St. George's flag, because that was the symbol of the Church of England and of Rome. Many of the Puritans had come to America to avoid the forms of worship used in the great English churches. Governor Endicott was for-

bidden to be governor or to hold any office in the gift of the king for a whole year.

On the other hand, different military companies and divisions of the country adopted special flags, as separate regiments in an army have different banners or ensigns. There is still preserved, in Bedford, Massachusetts, a Three-County Troop flag made in 1659, which is one of the oldest actual flags in the world. It is not so old, however, as the Cortez flag by more than one hundred and fifty years.

When the English colo-

JOHN ENDICOTT

nies or provinces had to combine to defend themselves against the French and their Indian allies, in what was known as the French and Indian War, the English colonists in America became most dissatisfied with their treatment at the hands of the Mother Country.

THE STAMP ACT DENOUNCED

THE STAMP ACT AND THE TEA TAX

JUST after the French and Indian War, England passed the Stamp Act, to make their American colonies pay money for certain stamps to put on their legal papers and documents— not for postage to carry them somewhere, as you put a stamp on a letter. All stamps were to be bought of English officers, and as the stamps were of no use whatever to those who had to pay for them, nearly every body in America regarded it as an unjust tax, so they refused to buy the stamps. They claimed that the English lawmakers were taxing the English in America when the people in this country had nothing to say about who should be taxed. No Americans were allowed to be members of the English lawmaking bodies, so they said this Stamp Act or stamp law was *"Taxation without representation."*

The people in America were so indignant about this unjust Stamp Act that it was repealed, or taken back—all but one little tax of "three-pence a pound" on tea. The English King and his advisers thought

A TAX GATHERER ROUTED

that would be such a little tax that the people in America would be ashamed to refuse to pay it.

The people in America used to sing a song or ballad of a great many stanzas about this tea tax. Here are a few verses of it:

> There was an old lady lived over the sea,
>   And she was an island queen;
> Her daughter lived off in a new countree
>   With an ocean of water between

The old lady's pockets were full of gold,
  But never contented was she;
So she called on her daughter to pay her a tax
  Of threepence a pound on her tea.

READING THE STAMP ACT IN BOSTON

"Now, mother, dear mother!" the daughter replied,
  "I shan't do the thing you ax;
I'm willing to pay a fair price for the tea—
  But never the threepenny tax!"

They knew very well that if they paid this small tax on tea it would not be long before the English Government would tax their coffee, then their sugar, then any or every thing they had to eat or to wear.

While these things were going on, George the Third, the slow, dull, selfish king of England, was surrounded by men who gave him bad advice. Besides, many of the governors, who had been sent from England to manage the affairs of the provinces, were stupid, mean and vain. They imposed upon and abused the people, often making wrong, and sometimes false, reports to the English Government about what was happening in America.

In addition to all this unfair treatment, Mother England did not try very hard to protect her children in America from their enemies, the French and the Indians. But poor old England had a war of her own on her hands, so she felt unable to help any of her colonies very much. That was one

KING GEORGE THE THIRD

reason why she thought she had to ins'st on her American children paying the small tax of "threepence a pound on her tea."

"THE BOSTON TEA PARTY"

IT was King James the First, known as "the fool king of England," who so badly treated his subjects who would not worship the way they did in the Church of England that he drove them out of the kingdom in the first place. They came as Pilgrims to America to live where they might worship God in any form they wished.

Then two other foolish kings, George the Second and George the Third, drove the people in America to revolt and take up arms against the Mother Country. One of the acts which brought about the war against England was the way the ships laden with taxed tea were received. In New York, Philadelphia, and cities farther south, the people refused to accept the tea. Philadelphia sent the tea ships back where they came from, without allowing them to be unloaded.

"THE BOSTON TEA PARTY"

In Boston they did more than this. The people held a great mass meeting and made a solemn protest against the injustice of any such tax. The English authorities paid no heed to this protest. So a band of fifty men dressed themselves up as Mohawk Indians and boarded the three English ships in Boston Harbor on the night of December

16th, 1773. Though many people witnessed this daring deed from the shore, it was all done in a quiet and orderly manner. The men in disguise broke open three hundred and forty-two chests of tea (valued at nearly one hundred thousand dollars) and threw all that tea into the water!

PAUL REVERE'S RIDE

"We will not consent to be taxed to pay for what we have nothing to say about or to do with. You are trying to make laws for us to obey, without giving us a chance to say whether they are just or not. It is not fair and we will not stand it any longer!"

This bold act made every body in America hold his breath, as it were, to see what England would do about it.

Meanwhile, Paul Revere, who had been one of the "Indians" in the "Tea Party," rode swiftly to New York and Philadelphia to give the warning and to call a convention of the leading men of all the colonies.

The suspense was intense. Every one felt that there might be a war with England, for the king and his ministers were now angry. Right

TARRING AND FEATHERING A LOYALIST

or wrong, they made up their minds to send troops and force the people in America to do as they had commanded.

After the soldiers came, Paul Revere went on his famous midnight ride to warn the farmers, the night before the first battle of the Revolution.

"To Arms! To Arms! The British are Coming"

THE BRITISH TROOPS IN BOSTON HARBOR, 1768
(The above picture was originally engraved by Paul Revere)

MOTHER AND DAUGHTER

SO long ago as 1645 the three colonies of Plymouth, Massachusetts Bay, and Connecticut began to arrange for a general defense. Miles Standish, the brave Plymouth captain, was one of the first men chosen to represent his colony in meetings for the union of the several colonies. This union grew, and other colonies came to be included, until the war with England made it necessary for all the colonies to unite for the defense of all, by means of an agreement called "The Act of Perpetual Union between the States." When they all combined and became independent, the former colonies or provinces were called States, and the United *Colonies* of America became the United *States* of America.

It is quite a lengthy story. Nothing shows the history of the long struggle better than the flags that were made and carried during those stormy days and months and years. As we have heard, poor old Mother England had so many troubles of her own that she paid very little heed to what her daughter across the wide water was doing. She thought her daughter had run away from home and that she was not worthy of much thought, anyway. In the midst of all her own cares, and wars, England forgot that her runaway daughter was really driven from home by a foolish king.

So, when people or troops or societies in her American colonies made up and carried different flags to please themselves, England paid very little attention to it, except when some one tore a piece out of her own flag, as you know Governor Endicott did, and was punished for it.

BATTLE SCENE ON LEXINGTON COMMON

So it is not at all surprising that England was angry when she heard of the heaving overboard of all that tea into Boston Harbor. When you come to think it all over, it was a bold, rather than a brave act. The tea did not belong to the king, but to private merchants who were acting within their rights and under royal authority. If a band of men nowadays should dress up like Indians and throw cargoes of tea overboard from ships in Boston, New York or Charleston harbor, the United States soldiers would be after them in short order. The Boston people were right in expecting trouble, for it soon came. British soldiers sailed across the sea with strict orders to put down the insurrection. They came, in the bright red coats which the people had learned to despise when Braddock and others had tried to fight the French and Indians in such a foolish way.

The boys and girls in Boston called the soldiers "lobster backs." You know a green lobster turns bright red when it is boiled. The children had been brought up to look with contempt on English soldiers. They hummed "Yankee Doodle" and "Chevy Chase" at them as they marched along, and the words they sang to those lively tunes were not friendly or complimentary to the "lobster backs." It made the soldiers angry, but, of course, they dared not hurt children, no matter how saucy they were.

Paul Revere had ridden to New York and Philadelphia to call a convention from all the colonies and was back in Boston long before the memorable night of April 18th, 1775, when he rode out from Boston to warn the farmers, shouting:

"Get up! Get up! The British are coming! The 'red coats' are coming!"

A few farmers were drawn up in line to meet the British soldiers at Lexington Green and at Concord Bridge. On the 19th of April, 1775, there were two little skirmishes which are now known as the first battle of the Revolution. The three northern counties along the coast of Massachusetts were named Essex, Middlesex and Suffolk. It was the troops of these counties that owned the old Three-Troop Flag already mentioned, that is still shown in the Library at Bedford, Middlesex County, Massachusetts. It is thought that this flag was brought by one of the "Minute Men" to Concord Bridge that day, and that was the banner referred to by Emerson, in the lines:

By the rude bridge that arched the flood,
  Their flag to April's breeze unfurled;
Here once the embattled farmers stood
  And fired the shot heard round the world.

THE DEFENCE OF BREED'S HILL. PRESCOTT IN THE REDOUBT

MANY FLAGS OF MANY KINDS

F LAG making ran riot among the English colonies in America after the Stamp Act was passed by the British Parliament, after the Tea Tax was announced, and especially after the "Boston Tea Party." Before that time the king's loyal subjects in those colonies were content with putting on their banners such solemn words as, *Qui transtulit sustinet*. After Massachusetts had adopted it for her coat-of-arms, this motto was copied for several New England flags. It is a Latin sentence which means: *He who brought* [us] *over* [the sea] *will sustain* [us.]

As many New England people did not like to have the red cross, they adopted "the king's colors," that is, a lion, a harp and other designs, all arranged in the shape of a shield in red, blue and yellow on a white flag. This was adopted in 1635. For nearly a hundred years

FIRST LIBERTY FLAG

before the Revolution the most popular flag in the colonies was red, with a red cross on a white field in the upper corner next the flagstaff. This field, sometimes white, sometimes blue, sometimes several colors, is called the canton—the name most used for this part in describing a flag. The people of Newbury, Massachusetts, in 1684, made a *green* flag with a red cross in a white canton. Some of the people preferred the regular red flag but without the cross, leaving the white canton blank.

In 1686, Governor Andros brought from England a white flag with a red cross on which was "emblazoned" a yellow crown and the king's initial, "R," for Rex, meaning "king." King Edward VII signs his name *"Edward R"*—for Edward Rex, which means King Edward. In South Carolina they had a beautiful blue flag with three crescents.

About the year 1700 was devised a blue flag with the red cross on the flag proper and with a green pine tree in the upper left-hand quarter of the white canton. It is said to be one of these Pine Tree flags which the continental troops carried at the Battle of Bunker Hill, June 17th, 1775. There is some disagreement as to the kind of flag that went into this great battle, but nearly all agree that there was a pine tree in the corner of it.

The Pine Tree seemed to be the favorite symbol of the forests and commerce of the country. Later, it was recommended by the Conti-mental Congress, for the colonial ships. A flag had to be adopted, as many ship-masters would not sail under the British flag, and any ship without an ensign was treated as a pirate. The Congress decided on the Pine Tree design at once. The flag which Lieut. John Paul Jones claimed to be the first authorized banner was that presented to the young naval officer by Colonel Gadsden. This was yellow, with a pine tree in the center, which had a rat-tlesnake coiled about its trunk. Above this tree were the words, "An Appeal to God," and beneath it, "Don't Tread on Me." Whatever the exact design of the flag may have been, and it is a disputed question, there is no doubt that John Paul Jones raised his naval flag to the masthead months before another flag, designed by Franklin, Washington and others, was adopted for the army at Cambridge.

PAUL JONES RAISING THE FLAG

The Pine Tree grew in size and impor-tance in its flag field until it became the only design in the whole white flag. Over this lone tree appeared the words, "An Appeal to Heaven." The Pine Tree came to be called the "Liberty" tree, and after-wards had the word "Liberty" above it. Later the phrases, "Liberty or Death," and "Lib-erty and Union" were used, and the tree had a rattlesnake coiled about its roots with *"Don't tread on me"* printed beneath. The motto on one New Hampshire flag, was quite matter-of-fact—*"Liberty, property, and no stamps!"*

ONE OF THE PINE TREE FLAGS

The rattlesnake was seized upon as the emblem of the American col-onies. This showed that the people's feelings toward the Mother

Country had become more spiteful than affectionate. They began to look upon the king as a tyrant, and the flags all had an aggressive tone.

One flag, early in 1776, showed thirteen red and white stripes, representing the thirteen colonies, with only a fat snake stretched diagonally across it, darting its forked tongue up in the corner where the canton would have been, and *"Don't tread on me"* printed across on the lowest white stripe.

Another banner appeared at this time bearing the war-cry, *"Conquer*

| A FLAG OF THE MINUTE MEN | A RATTLESNAKE FLAG | ANOTHER TYPE OF PINE TREE FLAG |

or Die." The same year there appeared a blue flag with a circle of thirteen stars representing the states. Also in 1776, at the battle of White Plains, was first seen a blue flag with a sword placed across a staff on which hung a liberty cap, this design being surrounded by the words, *"Liberty & Union." "Liberty or Death"* was a favorite flag motto, from the great speech of Patrick Henry, the Virginia patriot, ending with:

The war is actually begun. The next gale that sweeps from the north will bring to our ears the clash of resounding arms. Our brethren are already in the field. Why stand we here idle? What is it that gentlemen wish? What would they have? Is life so dear, or peace so sweet, as to be purchased at the price of chains and slavery? Forbid it, Almighty God! I know not what course others may take, but as for me, *give me liberty, or give me death!*

WEEDING OUT THE GARDEN OF THE FLAG

O F all the flags that came to light during those troubled and anxious years before the War for Independence, many of the banners seemed to express hatred of the Mother Country. Isn't it a good thing the rattlesnake was not the symbol adopted for our country's flag? There were many who wanted to make it a banner of *hate*.

They even made a flag with a big, long rattlesnake on it, of which the head was to stand for New England; one section was named "New York," another, "Virginia," and so on down to the tail, or "rattles," of which some one suggested there should be *thirteen,* the number of the colonies! It was thought *that* "13" might be an unlucky number for Old England! By the way, "13" ought to be a *lucky* number in the United States of America, because that was the number of the original colonies that won their independence, and there were just thirteen States at first. Also, Friday should be a lucky day in America, for Columbus discovered America on Friday, the 12th of October, 1492—and, besides, that little baby boy, George Washington, was born on Friday, the 22nd of February, 1732.

It was a fortunate thing that the rattlesnake flag was not adopted as the banner of our country. Think of having a snake flaunting over our homes and schoolhouses and public buildings! How would *you* like to wave your hat or your handkerchief and hurrah for a rattlesnake flag, as you do now for the Stars and Stripes? It was not mere "luck" that kept our fathers from adopting the rattlesnake for our standard. It was their good sense and their true hearts that prevented them from having a flag of hatred, and made them adopt in its place, the starry emblem we know so well as the banner of love. Hate does not do good things that last always, as love does; we hope our Flag and our country will endure forever.

Any of the other flags, fluttering in the breezes of 1775 and 1776, might better have been chosen for our national emblem than the rattlesnake. *"Liberty or Death,"* with its skull and cross-bones, sword and liberty cap, would have been only a little better. *"Conquer or Die"* was a better motto than *"Don't Tread on Me,"* but *"An Appeal to Heaven"* was an improvement on that, and the pine "Liberty" tree, with the motto, *"Liberty and Union,"* was still better. You can see, among all those flags, of love and hatred, that there were several that had thirteen red and white stripes, or thirteen white stars on a blue field, to represent the thirteen colonies. Our Flag's outliving all those others is a case of what the men of science call "the survival of the fittest." Wasn't it wonderful the way those beautiful stripes and stars came up and grew more and more lovely, like a magnificent flower in a garden, when all those hateful designs were pulled up and cast aside like so many weeds? Ours is a flag of love—not hate— the love that "suffereth long and is kind"—that "vaunteth not itself, is not puffed up, doth not behave itself unseemly,"— "beareth all things, believeth all things, hopeth all things, endureth all things."

Washington and his men, indeed, nearly all the people, had to bear all things, believe all things, hope all things, and endure all things, before they could bring our beautiful banner to its perfection and make it the Flag of the free and independent nation we are now so justly proud to call our own. The growth of the Flag even then was gradual and slow.

THE FLAG FRANKLIN AND HIS COMMITTEE DESIGNED

The first flag, devised by a committee of which Benjamin Franklin was chairman and adopted by the Continental Congress and General Washington, was not the Stars and Stripes, by any means. Its simple colored stripes tell a most interesting story. It shows that, even then, the colonies had no idea of separating from England. They were still loyal English people demanding the liberties and freedom from oppression that they believed their king and Parliament ought to grant to the faithful subjects beyond the sea. The flag that Franklin and the Congress devised for Washington proves this. Instead of having stars in the canton as they are now, they had the British flag—the English Cross of St. George, in red, and the Scotch cross of St. Andrew, in white, placed one over the other, on a blue canton. With this design they had thirteen red and white stripes, to show that the thirteen colonies were banded together but still loyal to the old flag if the king and his counsellors would grant them the liberty due to all Englishmen, allow them to be represented in the English Parliament and have a

READING THE DECLARATION OF INDEPENDENCE TO THE ARMY   39

voice in the affairs of government, especially in the management of their own matters.

When this flag was raised over the garrison at Cambridge, Massachusetts, with appropriate ceremonies, by Washington and the Flag Committee, it was greeted with thirteen cheers and thirteen guns—that is, a cannon was fired thirteen times.

This flag was displayed by Washington at the head of the colonial army, in Cambridge, just across the river from Boston, on New Year's Day,* 1776, six months before the Continental Congress, in Philadelphia, voted to adopt the Declaration of Independence. The British, when they saw the new banner, seemed to understand that it meant that the colonies would yield after all, for Washington several days later, January 4th, 1776, wrote to his military secretary, in part, as follows:

We gave great joy to them (the British in Boston) without knowing or intending it; for on that day, the day which gave being to the new army, but before the proclamation came to hand, we had hoisted the Union flag in compliment to the United Colonies. But behold! it was received in Boston as a token of the deep impression the [king's] speech had made upon us, and as a signal of submission. So we hear, by a person out of Boston, last night. By this time, I presume, they begin to think it strange that we have not made a formal surrender of our lives!

THE FIRST FLAG OF THE UNITED STATES

BUT King George soon learned that Washington and his army were not going to plead for their lives! The British were surprised to see how much in earnest all the people were— "the peasants," as they called them. The soldiers from across the sea were highly indignant because they were brought over here to fight the "peasantry." But when the "peasantry" had routed them with great slaughter, and made the "red coats" run all the way from Concord and Lexington back to Boston, they began to see the difference between the peasants of Europe and the farmers of America. For the farmers in this country, even at that time, read and thought, and knew when their rights were trampled on. It was the American

* This "Grand Union" flag was first raised on the 1st of January, in spite of the fact that several authorities give the date as January 2nd.

SERGEANT JASPER RECOVERING THE ENSIGN OF SOUTH CAROLINA AT SULLIVAN ISLAND

farmer that defeated the English king and forced him to yield us our independence.

If King George had only known it, he might even then have stopped the war by granting justice to the colonists, but his bad advisers told him the stupid "peasants" were much frightened and about to surrender. But there was one British leader who was able to see that the Americans had rights which even England was bound to respect.

This man was the first William Pitt, Earl of Chatham, the great orator and statesman, who had spoken in behalf of the Americans before, against taxation, and other unjust laws. In a fiery speech, in the House of Lords, at the opening of Parliament, November 18th, 1777, Lord Chatham said, with deep feeling:

CHATHAM'S MONUMENT IN WESTMINSTER ABBEY

If I were an American, as I am an Englishman, while a foreign troop was landed in my country, I would never lay down my arms—never! —NEVER! —NEVER!

But it was too late then—over sixteen months after the American colonists had been driven to draw up and sign the Declaration of Independence. Within six months after Washington and his staff had raised the United Colonies flag over the garrison at Cambridge, the Continental Congress met again in Philadelphia to adopt the grand Declaration, and after that first Fourth of July, the great Liberty Bell, over Independence Hall, rang out clear and strong, to "proclaim liberty throughout the land unto all the inhabitants thereof."

The people were no longer satisfied to fight for rights which they

WHERE THE FIRST CONGRESS MET, PHILADELPHIA 43

found, to their sorrow, that England would never allow. Through those long and bitter years they had learned that the only way to get what England would not grant was to "help themselves" to it. The only course left to them was to fight England, cut loose from her altogether and govern themselves, which they felt that they were capable of doing. But could they fight England and win? That was a grave question. They were brave and angry enough to try. It might be a long struggle— but Liberty was worth suffering and dying for. The Declaration of Independence is the grandest state paper in the world on human government. Its remonstrances and appeals exhibited the highest abilities as well as the loftiest patriotism. It was signed by fifty-six men from the old Thirteen States, all of high rank, and great worth and talents.

THE LIBERTY BELL

The Declaration, adopted by all the delegates of all the late Colonies, now formed the Thirteen United States of America.

So another flag was needed—or a real Liberty Flag. In June, 1776, only a few weeks before the great Declaration, a committee of three persons, General Washington, Robert Morris (who afterwards became the money manager of the Revolution) and Colonel George Ross, called on Mrs. Ross, the widow of Colonel Ross's nephew, to have a banner made. The members of the committee had evidently availed themselves of the advice of Dr. Benjamin Franklin, for he was interested in flags and had been chairman of the previous Flag Committee. Washington and his friends seem to have had a pretty distinct idea of what they wanted.

It has been shown how the idea of the Stars and Stripes had been growing up among all the queer designs that had been flung to the breezes during those years of turmoil and trouble with the Mother Country. The thirteen colonies had often been represented, on sea and land, by thirteen stripes, and sometimes by thirteen white stars in a blue sky or field. These stars were generally five-pointed. The Committee seems to have agreed upon placing the thirteen stars—in a circle, in a blue canton. But Washington, in his drawing, had made the stars six-pointed, it is said, because he wanted to make the stars *different* from those in his own coat-of-arms, which were five-pointed! It is

THE BIRTH OF THE FLAG 45

often stated that Washington secured the design for our Flag from his own book-plate! No doubt Franklin suggested this, also. But there had been several flags made of thirteen stripes, and quite a number of star standards appeared about this time. If his coat-of-arms had really resembled the flag, that would have been the very reason why Washington would *not* have allowed it to be copied. He was not that kind of a man. There is nothing that can be quoted from what Washington ever said or wrote, of all that is left to us, that even hints at such an idea. Indeed much that he wrote seems rather to contradict the notion of his copying his coat-of-arms. Here is his own sentiment, expressed some time afterwards, about the first of all the Stars and Stripes:

We take the star from Heaven, the red from our Mother Country, separating it by white stripes, thus showing that we have separated from her, and the white stripes shall go down to posterity representing liberty.

BETSY ROSS AND THE FLAG

MRS. ELIZABETH ROSS was an attractive young widow—she was twenty-four years of age when the flag was made—who lived in a little house in Arch Street, Philadelphia. She was supporting herself by carrying on an upholstery business. Every body loved her and called her Betsy. This was the nickname for Elizabeth. She was famous for her skill with the needle and for her good taste and good sense, as well as for her business ability. She had met John Ross in the upholstery shop where they both worked and was disowned by the Friends after running away to be married to him. The Quakers also expelled from the Society of Friends all who had anything to do with war. Those Friends who had helped in the War of the Revolution afterwards organized a society called "Free Quakers."

When General Washington and his secret or self-appointed committee needed some one to make up the flag they had planned, they naturally went to the bright and skillful young "Widow Ross," as she was sometimes called. Besides, Betsy was a niece, by marriage. of Colonel Ross, one of the so-called committee. Washington laid the design before the blooming young woman, with his accustomed gallantry.

When Mrs. Ross saw the six-pointed star in his drawing, she took a piece of paper, folded it, made one clip of the scissors, unfolded it and smilingly held up a perfect five-pointed star.

The men were delighted with her deftness and skill, and felt that the bright little woman was just the right person to whom to entrust the making of the wonderful new flag. They told her what they desired —thirteen red and white stripes, with the red at top and bottom of the flag, which would make seven red stripes, and six white. The canton to be a blue square, extending from the top down over the seven bars and stopping at the eighth, a white stripe. In this blue field was a circle of thirteen white stars. The description given by the Congress was of "a constellation," or a group of stars. The story is told that John Adams wished to have the stars arranged in the form of the star-group, Lyra, which is the shape of a lyre or harp, as there were just thirteen stars in that constellation. But they could not arrange it to look well, so they decided on the circle of stars. As there is no end to a circle, they hoped the new nation they were trying to organize would also be without end—that it would live until the end of time.

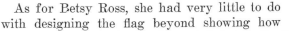

THE ORIGINAL BETSY
ROSS FLAG

As for Betsy Ross, she had very little to do with designing the flag beyond showing how easily she could make the five-pointed stars for it. But she followed the directions given her by Washington and his committee, and made the first flag of the United States of America.

Wasn't that glory enough? She did her work so well that she made all the official flags for ten years or more. That was her secret. *She only did her work well,* and her good name and lovely face have been framed in history and draped with her flag beside that of Washington, and this sweet story shall be told "in memorial of her" as long as the Stars and Stripes shall continue to wave.

The little house in which Betsy Ross lived, now No. 239 Arch Street, Philadelphia, is still kept as it was when she lived there alone after the death of her husband. It is called "the Flag House," and "the Betsy Ross House." This historic house has been saved to the country as a memorial through the patriotic and highly successful management of Charles H. Weisgerber, the painter of the celebrated picture illustrating the birth of our Flag.

The flag was not approved by Congress for about a year. Washington's committee must have reported in due time, but Congress had even more important business on hand than the approval of a flag, for they had to pilot the new Ship of State over shoals and past rocks and through rapids before it could fly a flag at all.

Finally, after many flags had been made and displayed, Congress adopted the flag designed by Washington, Morris, Ross and Franklin, and made by Betsy Ross, on the 14th of June, 1777, with the following resolution:

Resolved, that the flag of the thirteen United States be thirteen stripes, alternate red and white; that the union (canton) be thirteen stars, white in a blue field, representing a new constellation.

So the fourteenth day of June, the day on which the first United States Flag was adopted, is now known as Flag Day, which is celebrated yearly all over the United States.

THE FIRST AMERICAN FLAG OVER A FORT

No tyrant hath claimed that flag for his own;
Its bright folds were never unfurled
To flatter or shelter the glare of a throne;
That banner was born for the world.

THE first time the real Stars and Stripes ever floated over a fort on land was August 3d, 1777. A commanding lieutenant named Gansevoort, at Fort Stanwix (later called Fort Schuyler), where Rome, New York, now stands, saw in the *Pennsylvania Gazette,* a description of the new flag just adopted by the Continental Congress, and set about making the authorized banner. He asked a young woman to find him some red cloth.

There was no place in a fort where bunting could be bought, but a soldier's wife was found who had a bright red petticoat, which she said she was glad to give for such a good purpose. The white cotton, for the white stripes and the stars, was torn from ammunition shirts, and the blue for the canton was cut from an old army cloak, so it did not take long for the lieutenant and his good assistant, aided by a drummer boy, to put the colors together. They had to sew a square of blue on each side, in the upper left-hand corner and stitch on six white strips of cotton for the stripes, on each side equal distances apart, letting the red stripes show between. Then they sewed thirteen white stars in a

HOW THE CLOTH FOR THE FIRST FLAG WAS MADE

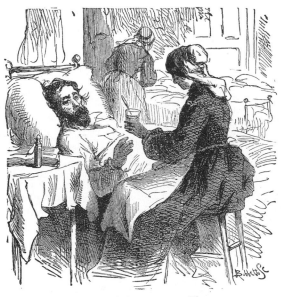

WOMAN'S WORK IN THE WAR

circle on the blue field or canton.

This petticoat flag was the first American flag to wave over an actual engagement. But it probably looked more beautiful to the brave little garrison in Fort Stanwix, waving there in the breeze, than the most costly silk flag you ever saw. Wasn't that woman proud of her petticoat? Wasn't she glad she had made a sacrifice for the sake of the Flag? By the way, women help and make as great sacrifices as men for the country and for the right, in times of war and in times of peace, too. Even Washington had to go and get the aid of Betsy Ross before the first flag of our Union could be made. Lieutenant Gansevoort could never have had the great honor of raising the first flag at Fort Stanwix but for the help of two women whose names we do not know—the one who sacrificed her red woollen skirt in her country's cause, and the other who helped him make a banner of it.

Even in war-time, the "boys" who go to the front, to fight, and perhaps die, are no more brave than the mothers, sisters, sweethearts, wives and daughters who work and suffer in silence and sleepless anxiety, then have to bear the anguish of the deepest grief the human heart can know, followed by lifelong loss and loneliness.

HOW A WOMAN DEFENDED THE FLAG

But let us go back to our Flag. There were only a few men in Fort Stanwix. They "held the fort" bravely against Lieutenant St. Leger and his Indian allies until help came. It was a struggle of about three weeks, against British and Indians, who came and were kept at bay by the brave garrison within, but they held out nobly. Not only this but the soldiers of the fort made successful raids among the allies, driving them away. So the first time our flag waved over a land engagement it was the banner of victory.

THE STAR SPANGLED BANNER

THE Flag remained as Washington's committee and Betsy Ross made it, with thirteen stripes and thirteen stars—the stars being arranged in a circle, and sometimes in rows, as there was no exact form prescribed—for eighteen years. The thirteen original States, in the order of their admission to the Union, were: Delaware, Pennsylvania, New Jersey, Georgia, Connecticut, Massachusetts, Maryland, South Carolina, New Hampshire, Virginia, New York, North Carolina and Rhode Island.

But Vermont was added to the Union in 1791, and Kentucky in 1792, so it became necessary to add these stars to the galaxy of the original thirteen. This was done in 1795, placing two more stars in the blue canton, and adding two stripes, one red and one white, making fifteen stars and fifteen stripes; these stripes, of course, had to be made narrower, for the width of the new flag was just the same as before.

THE FLAG ABOUT WHICH
THE "STAR SPANGLED
BANNER" WAS WRITTEN

The bill providing for this change was approved and signed by President Washington on the 13th of January, 1794. It read as follows:

An act making alterations in the flag of the United States. *Be it enacted, etc.,* That from and after the first of May, One Thousand seven hundred and ninety-five, the flag of the United States be fifteen stripes, alternate red and white, and that the union be fifteen stars, white in a blue field.

This fifteen-stripe flag, with its fifteen stars, sometimes in a circle, sometimes arranged in the form of a large star, and sometimes, placed in rows, remained for twenty-three years, or until 1818. This, then, was the standard which floated over land and sea all through the second war with England, commonly known as "the War of 1812."

It was this flag which inspired Francis Scott Key, a young lawyer of the city of Washington, to write his spirited song, "The Star Spangled Banner," which was adapted to the older tune, "Anacreon in Heaven."

The British had taken Washington city, driven out President Madison and the rest of the government officials, and burned the White

House and the Capitol, leaving only their blackened walls. Young Key had a friend who was a prisoner on board a British warship. He went, under a white flag, or flag of truce, to visit his friend just as the British were proceeding against Baltimore. They took Mr. Key with them and kept him prisoner till after the engagement, as they could not allow him to return and report what he had seen on a British ship. The garrison in Fort McHenry stoutly resisted the attack. The young American was naturally very anxious to have the fort hold out. Until almost dark he strained his eyes to see if the dear Flag was still waving

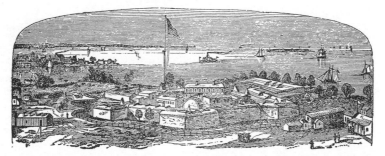

THE FLAG OVER FORT MCHENRY: INSPIRATION OF "THE STAR SPANGLED BANNER"

over the fort. The bombardment was kept up, and rockets and bombs were discharged nearly all that night, as he describes in his poem:

> And the rockets' red glare, the bombs bursting in air,
> Gave proof through the night that our Flag was still there.

"Does the Star Spangled Banner yet wave?" was the anxious question the American prisoner asked himself all night long. Before daylight the firing ceased, and Key was almost ill with anxiety lest the brave little garrison had been compelled to give up the fight.

In the gray dawn of the morning he could just discern a flag floating over the fort. But he could not see it distinctly. Which was it— the red and blue "Union Jack" of Great Britain, or our own dear "Flower of Freedom?" While he was straining his eyes, trying to distinguish, the sun rose and his heart leaped with joy to see "that our Flag was still there!"

From his pocket he took a letter he had lately received and, on the

Washington Crossing the Delaware

blank pages of the sheets wrote the immortal lines which inspire our vast audiences to rise and stand while singing—the thrilling song which closes with:

> Then conquer we must when our cause it is just,
> And this be our motto, "In God is our trust,"
> And the Star Spangled Banner in triumph shall wave
> O'er the land of the free and the home of the brave.

That old flag—the first to be called the Star Spangled Banner—is still preserved, torn and tattered as it was on that memorable day and

night, September 13th, 1814, while Francis Scott Key watched and listened in the agony of suspense. He lived nearly thirty years after this thrilling experience. There is a statue in his honor standing in Golden Gate Park, San Francisco.

Before the great battle of Lake Erie, September 10th, 1813, Commodore Perry hoisted a flag bearing the words, *"Don't give up the ship,"* over a

The Star-Spangled banner.

O say! can you see by the dawn's early light
What so proudly we hail'd at the twilight's last gleaming.
Whose broad stripes and bright stars through the clouds of the fight.
O'er the ramparts we watch'd were so gallantly streaming?
And the rocket's red glare – the bomb bursting in air
Gave proof through the night that our flag was still there?
O say, does that star-spangled banner yet wave
O'er the land of the free & the home of the brave? —

J. F. Key

THE FIRST STANZA OF "THE STAR SPANGLED BANNER" AS KEY WROTE IT

ship, the *Lawrence,* which he had named for his friend Captain James Lawrence, who was shot on board his ship, the *Cheasapeake.* Lawrence's last words were: "Don't give up the ship!" This was the battle after which Perry reported his victory in the famous dispatch: "We have met the enemy and they are ours."

By 1818, many new States had been added to the Union, and it was found that to make a new stripe for each new State would be next to impossible, unless the stripes should be narrowed down almost to "pin stripes," so it was decided, after years of discussion, that the number of *stripes should remain thirteen,* the number of the first States when the Union was founded, and the *stars should show the number of States.*

No form or design was set for the arrangement of the stars. These were placed in rows, and every time a new State star was added a rearrangement was required.

"REPRESENTING A NEW CONSTELLATION"

WHEN Franklin, Washington, Mr. Robert Morris, Colonel Ross and the Continental Congress planned our Flag, they meant to have the stars arranged in a "constellation." This was distinctly shown in the official order for making the Flag. Betsy Ross, under the direction of Washington and other members of the Flag Committee, placed the thirteen stars in a circle. How much more beautiful that flag was than, for instance, the next flag adopted, with fifteen stripes and fifteen stars, in five rows of three each.

The other nations used to laugh at our patchwork quilt flag, evidently made by a woman, they said, and without any knowledge of heraldry, or the art of flag-making—with the stars in straight misfit rows set in against the stripes. But heraldry is the art of monarchy and of aristocracy, so it was especially fitting that the American flag should not conform to rules laid down by the effete monarchies of Europe. Of course, England tried to "poke" fun at our flag with its thirteen stripes and thirteen stars. In 1783, when the first vessel flying the United States colors appeared in the River Thames, this "extraordinary event" was announced to the British ministers in Parliament,

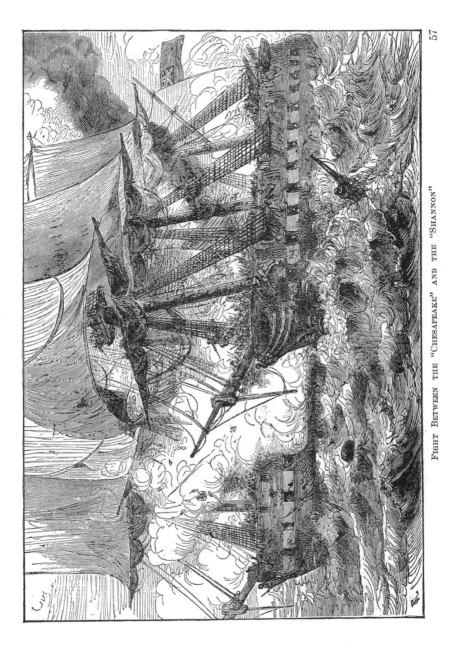

FIGHT BETWEEN THE "CHESAPEAKE" AND THE "SHANNON"

as none of the harbor or custom-house officers knew what to do about it. The *Political Magazine* records that *"the ministers remained silent!"* An article appeared in the *London Chronicle* of the 7th of February, 1783, making all manner of ridicule of the flag and its repeating the number thirteen. Here is part of this "humorous" description. It will be remembered that Washington and his army, and afterward the people of the United States, were referred to in England as "rebels":

There is a vessel in the harbor with a very strange flag. Thirteen is a number peculiar to the rebels. A party of naval prisoners lately returned from Jersey say that the rations among the rebels are thirteen dried clams a day. . . . It takes thirteen Congress paper dollars to equal one shilling sterling. Polly [General "Mad Anthony"] Wayne was just thirteen hours in subduing Stony Point, and thirteen seconds in leaving it. Every well-organized rebel household has thirteen children, all of whom expect to be major-generals, or members of the high and mighty congress of the thirteen United States when they attain the age of thirteen years. Mr. Washington has thirteen teeth in each jaw, and thirteen toes on each foot, the extra ones having grown since that wonderful declaration of independence; and Mrs. Washington has a tomcat with thirteen yellow rings around his tail, and his flaunting it suggested to the Congress the same number of stripes for the rebel flag.

But in spite of the silence of the British ministers and the ribald jokes in the newspapers, the flag of the "Thirteen Stripes" was treated with due respect. The people of London could hardly be expected to see anything beautiful in the victorious Stars and Stripes. As has been stated, thirteen should be a lucky number for all true Americans.

The original design of Washington, Franklin and others of the fathers and heroes of the Declaration of Independence to group the stars in a constellation in the blue sky of the flag was beautiful, artistic, full of meaning, and conformed to the recognized rules of flag-making among the nations of the world. It was afterward, when so many States were added to the Union that the stars were crowded into straight rows, at "sixes and sevens," then sevens and eights, that the beauty and symmetry of the blue "union" or canton were lost. Fortunately, there is no legal or prescribed arrangement of the stars more binding than that of the original order, *"representing a new constellation."*

So it is not too late now to make a combination of the stars in such a group or constellation as shall enhance the beauty of what is already the loveliest flag in all the world. This can be done in such a way as to make the stars record the thrilling history of our country. For instance, the thirteen original States might be shown in the center of the blue sky in the form of a six-pointed star. This six-pointed star would tell that at first there were thirteen British colonies—for the English star is six-pointed—that united to form our thirteen original States. There might be placed about that star a circle of twenty-five stars, representing the States of which Colorado, added during the Centennial year, 1876, was the last admitted. This circle of stars, surrounding and defending the original thirteen, would mean just what Washington, Franklin and the others meant by the circle of stars in the flag they directed Betsy Ross to make: that our Union was to be without end, as Daniel Webster afterwards expressed it in the greatest of all his great speeches—"Liberty and Union, now and forever, one and inseparable."

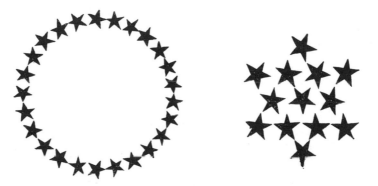

The star and circle would thus provide for the thirty-eight States of the first hundred years of United States history. Outside the circle the remaining stars could be in the form of a larger circle, or scattered, some nearer, some farther from the outer edges of the canton, as in a constellation in the sky.

This arrangement, besides fulfilling the design of the Father of his Country and the framers of the Constitution, symbolizes the history of the United States. This being more beautiful and according to republican rules of flag-making, would make it easy to add the star of each new State without having to disarrange and rearrange the whole canton, as is now the case. The cantons of different flags one sees every-where display sad lack of order. "Order is Heaven's first law," and in nothing should this high law be observed more than in the setting

of the stars in our country's standard. This arrangement is suggested merely as a great improvement over the prevailing want of order. It may be that some loyal man or woman, boy or girl, will suggest a better solution of this great problem.

BRITISH OFFICERS IMPRESSING AMERICAN SAILORS

THE FIRST STARS AND STRIPES OVER A SCHOOL-HOUSE

FLYING the flag over all the school-houses in the land is a recent custom, but as long ago as the War of 1812 the standard of our country was set up over the little old log school-house on Catamount Hill, one of the Berkshires, in western Massachusetts. This is believed to be the first flag that ever floated over a school-house in the United States. The War of 1812 was declared June 18th, 1812. This war was necessary because Mother England was so slow in learning that her child across the sea was quite able to take care of herself. As a mother sometimes tries, after her daughter is married, to manage the affairs of the young household, so England showed herself unwilling to let the United States go alone. The Mother Country made herself obnoxious by claiming the right to search American ships for runaway British seamen. Sometimes the English took American sailors off our warships and "impressed" them into English service, that is, made them work and fight for England against their will. This was even worse than the English tax on American tea, which had brought on the first war. Just as "a man's house is his castle," the Americans maintained that no one had a right to break in upon their ships and turn things topsy-turvy, hunting for men or anything else. Besides, if the British were permitted to search for sailors or soldiers, what was to prevent their "breaking and entering" anywhere, at any time they chose, under that or some other pretext? "Give England an inch," they said, "and she will take an ell," so they decided not to give one inch.

On the other hand, here was England's idea of American *dependence* (instead of the *in*dependence she had fought eight years for and won) as expressed by Lord Liverpool, a leader in the British Parliament:

America ought to have looked to England as a guardian power, to which she was indebted, not only for her comfort, not only for her rank in the scale of civilization, but for her very existence.

The Americans could not see the matter in that light, so there had to be another war to teach England the rest of her lesson as to what American independence really meant. Out of the six men who went to this war from the township of Colrain, Massachusetts, five were from Catamount Hill, where patriotism ran high. That is how the flag came to fly over the old school-house on Catamount Hill. Mrs. Fanny Bowen Shippee, a relative of those who took part in the flag-making and flag-raising, wrote a quaint ballad, telling the homely story of the first flag over a school-house in the United States. She told how—

> Mrs. Rhoda Shippee, who stood for the right,
> Gave cloth for the stars and the field of pure white;
> It was wove on her loom, and hatchelled from tow,
> And of beautiful finish, as white as the snow.
> And Mrs. Lois Shippee for the "union" gave blue,
> Which she spun, colored, and wove—it was lovely to view.

Then the ballad goes on to tell us:

> And they planted that staff, and they worked with a will,
> 'Twas as straight as an arrow, and as trim as a quill,
> And all the people were there from "the Hill."
> They stood there in groups a-waiting to see
> That emblem so grand—the Flag of the Free!

They made no long speeches, they made no long prayer,
But of those who were gifted a plenty were there.
There was no sounding of trumpet, no beating of drum,
No tramping or marching, no firing of gun.
But the farmers were there, attired in their frocks,
And plenty of children, without slippers or socks.

In June, 1903, the Catamount Hill Association, after thorough search, not finding any earlier school-house flag in the whole country, met and set up a block of native stone on which was carved the following inscription:

> THE FIRST U. S. FLAG
> RAISED OVER A PUBLIC SCHOOL
> WAS FLOATED IN MAY, 1812
> FROM A LOG SCHOOL-HOUSE
> WHICH STOOD ON THIS SPOT

THE FLAG AND THE SCHOOL

THE first Flag to be raised over a grammar school was unfurled May 11th, 1861, at the beginning of the Civil War, by Sylvander Hutchinson, principal of the Fifth Street Grammar School, at New Bedford, Massachusetts. This example was soon followed in other towns in Massachusetts, New Hampshire, New York, and scattered in a few instances all over the North. But it was more than twenty years after the Civil War before the present custom became general. A New York newspaper, in 1889, began to advocate the flying of the United States flag over the public schools and other public buildings every day. *The Youth's Companion,* published in Boston, took the matter up in 1888, and taught the youth and their elders, all over the land, lessons in practical patriotism. Mr. J. B. Upham's Pledge of Allegiance, the one now commonly used, was repeated by more than twelve million pupils at the National School Celebration, October 21st, 1892, as a direct result of this grand movement.

As the Flag waves over the Capitol at Washington and all the State Capitols, while the legislators are in session, so the national colors are flying over the school-houses of the United States while the future citizens, legislators, members of Congress, and even Presidents to be, are in school session.

It is highly fitting that the Flag should fly over our school-houses, for the Public School is one of the grandest of all American institutions. It is on these schools that our liberties, other American institutions, and even the government itself, rely for their future life. So, what better knowledge can be taught in American schools than lessons in patriotism—true love of the Flag which means so much to every man, woman and child in the United States? It means a great deal to foreigners, too, for people of other lands are flocking to our shores by millions, because of the liberty which all Americans enjoy. They appreciate our freedom the more because they have been denied it. Sometimes we do not value our greatest gifts and blessings, just because we have always had them, but if we had to do without them a while we would soon learn what they mean to us, as, when we have been deprived of water for days, we appreciate what a real blessing a good drink of water is. So with freedom. It is sometimes stated that the truest and most loyal citizens of the United States are those who, or whose fathers, have come from distant lands where they have been deprived of the liberties which seem as common in America as the water we drink or the air we breathe.

The same is true of education. American children do not appreciate the privilege of going to school and learning, because that, too, seems "as free as the air." Many of our parents, who have never had such advantages, are the more anxious that their children shall have the very chances in life that they themselves have been denied.

So it is not only in our own country that the American flag looks beautiful. In every foreign country the people look upon it as the banner of freedom, of the rights of all, of a chance to work for good pay, of the right to have and to keep what they have earned, of the right to rise in the social scale in the country where all are considered equal as to "life, liberty, and the pursuit of happiness." In many other countries this is not the case. People who are born poor are kept down—they are oppressed. In Russia, and other countries, the farmers are very poor and ignorant. They are almost serfs or slaves. In Ireland the conditions are so hard to bear that many Irish people come to America and become our best and most successful citizens, often tak-

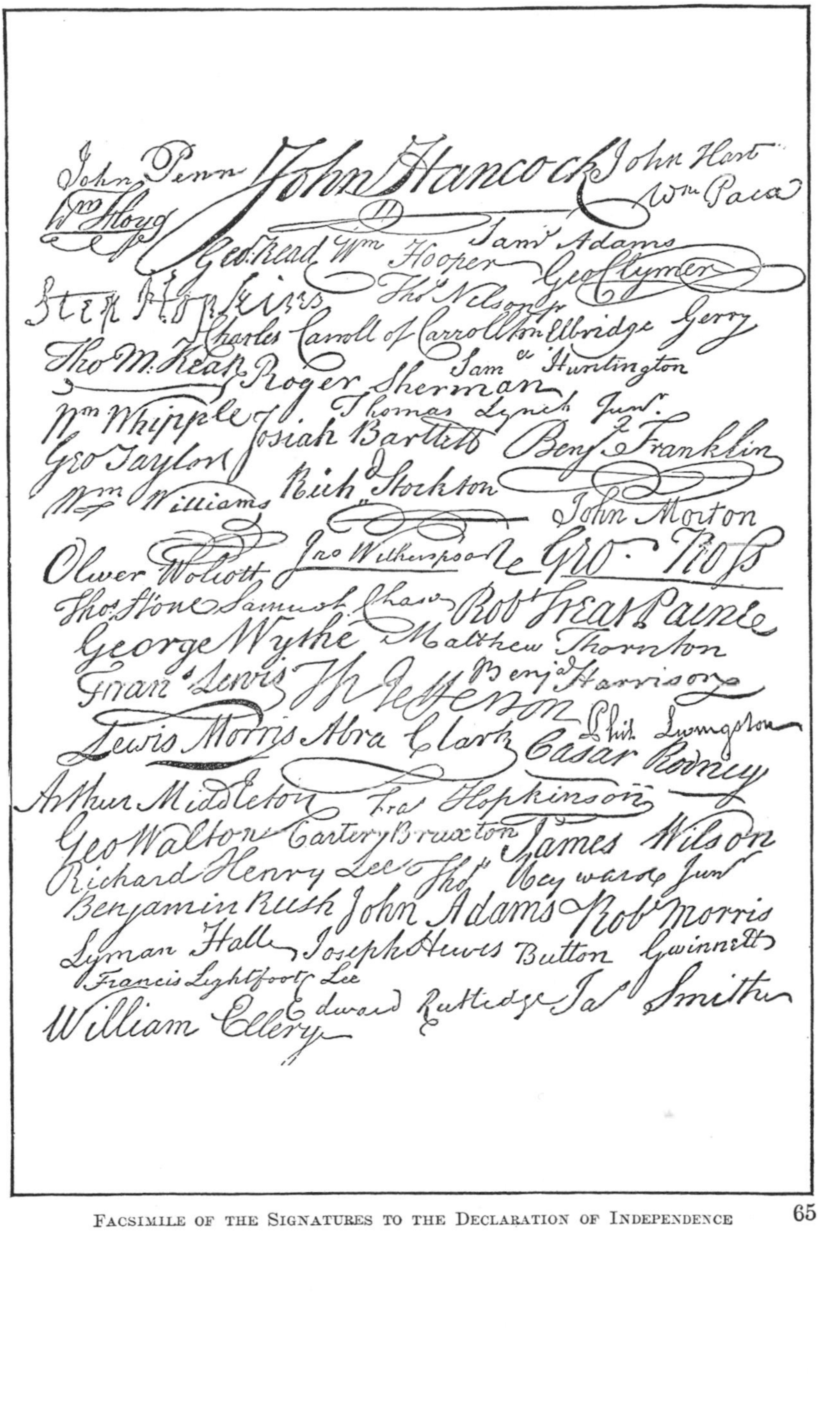

FACSIMILE OF THE SIGNATURES TO THE DECLARATION OF INDEPENDENCE

ing a lead in the affairs of government. In Germany all the young men are "pressed into the emperor's service," that is, they have to serve several years in the German army whether they wish to or not. Sometimes the emperor requires the best years of a young man's life, the very years he needs to establish himself in business, or to support his aged parents or his younger brothers and sisters. For those who, of their own free will, choose a military training, all this is well enough, but for those who do not care to be soldiers, and sincerely feel that a higher duty calls them in another direction, it is very hard. In America men are allowed to do things, as long as those things are not in themselves wrong, of their own free will and accord.

In other countries there are different reasons why the people are so glad to come to America and live their own free, unhampered lives under the Stars and Stripes. That is why a million people land on our shores, mostly at New York, every year. These people go west and are scattered far and wide, yet many of them are huddled together in the large cities. Some of them, but not so many as one might think, compared with the vast multitudes of foreigners who are constantly coming, have become embittered against the governments of their home countries. This makes it all the more necessary and a better thing to teach the children of these dissatisfied people the true inner beauties of the Stars and Stripes. With every wave the Stars and Stripes seems to be saying to all the world those familiar words of the fathers in the wonderful Declaration of Independence:

We hold these truths to be self-evident,—that all men are created equal; that they are endowed by their Creator with certain unalienable rights; that among these are life, liberty, and the pursuit of happiness.

THE FLAG IN THE SCHOOL

SINCE the Flag is floating above the school-houses all over the land, and in Porto Rico, Hawaii, the Philippines and other far-off isles of the sea, it is right and proper that there should be exercises inside the school-houses.

The Woman's Relief Corps first introduced the flag salute into the public schools, in 1886, for the sake of giving many little foreigners

a Declaration by the Representatives of the UNITED STATES OF AMERICA, in General Congress assembled.

When in the course of human events it becomes necessary for one people to dissolve the political bands which have connected them with ... and to assume among the powers of the earth the ... equal

...which the laws of nature & of nature's god entitle them, a decent respect to the opinions of mankind requires that they should declare the cause which impel them to the separation.

We hold these truths to be self-evident, that all men are created equal ... that ... they are endowed by their creator with ... equal ... rights, that ... among these are ... life, & liberty, & the pursuit of happiness; that to secure these rights, go—

THE FIRST DRAFT OF THE DECLARATION OF INDEPENDENCE IN JEFFERSON'S HANDWRITING AND WITH HIS OWN CORRECTIONS. (From the original, preserved in Washington.)

in New York City their first lessons in loyalty to the Flag of the country of their parents' adoption. Now certain daily exercises are repeated in the broken accents of the dusky peoples of distant lands lately taken under the protection of the United States Government and Flag. Everywhere—in Pennsylvania and the Philippines, in Alabama and Alaska—the flag drill is much the same.

After the pupils are assembled in school, the principal or teacher gives the signal, every child rises in his or her place. While the Flag is borne from the door to the teacher's stand, each pupil gives it the military salute, and repeats this pledge:

> *I pledge allegiance to my Flag, and to the Republic for which it stands,*
> *One nation, indivisible, with liberty and justice for all.*

In saying the words, *"to my Flag,"* each pupil finishes the salute by pointing the right hand gracefully, palm upward, toward the flag, holding it in that position until the end of the pledge. Then all hands drop to the side together. While still standing, the whole school sings, in unison, the national hymn, "America."

In some schools where the children are too small to repeat and understand the words "allegiance," "indivisible," etc., in the above pledge, this form is given:

> We give our heads and our hearts to God and our country—
> One Country, one Nation, one Flag.

The great strength of our national hymn is in that word *my*—*"My* country, 'tis of thee,"* which makes the heart-appeal even stronger than if it were written, *"Our* country." Some teacher, realizing the sense of personal responsibility inherent in the first person singular (for no child can really pledge for any but himself alone), has given the following:

> I give *my* head, *my* heart, *my* hand to *my* country,—
> One Nation, one Language, one Flag.

Some principals have the pledge salute repeated in concert on special occasions, but for the regular daily drill the ordinary military salute is given in silence. This act of reverence is very impressive. The Flag is brought to its station usually in front of the teacher's desk. At a given signal the right hand of each pupil is raised, palm downward, to a horizontal position against the forehead, and held there while the Flag is "dipped" and returned to its upright position. Then, at a second signal, the hand falls to the side and each pupil takes his seat.

Sometimes, in schools largely made up of children of many nations, there is a march and a "Flag Salute." A boy or girl carries the flag, followed by a color-guard of several boys or girls, or both, led by a drummer. The children take their places in rows and all sing together —often the song, "Flag of the Free," to the tune of the Wedding March from *Lohengrin*.

After this the bearer of the colors plants the Flag on the platform, and all the children join in repeating this beautiful pledge of

ALLEGIANCE TO THE FLAG:

Flag of our great Republic, inspirer in battle, guardian of our homes, whose stars and stripes stand for bravery, purity, truth, and union,

WE SALUTE THEE!

We, the natives of distant lands, who find rest under thy folds, do pledge our hearts, our lives, and our sacred honor, to love and protect thee, our Country, and the liberty of the American people forever.

In saying, "We salute thee," the children give the military salute. While pledging their "hearts, lives and sacred honor" to the country, they cross their hands upon their breasts, and when they come to the final words, "the American people forever," they all lift their hands as if to call Heaven to witness their solemn pledge.

It is a touching spectacle, to see little Chinese, Japanese, Turks, Armenians, Hungarians, Poles—children of "every nation under Heaven," pledging themselves with accents peculiar to the lands of their birth, giving their hearts and lives to their new country, the "Sweet Land of Liberty!"

NOTE.—For drills, prose "pieces," poetry, etc., for declamations and exercises for Flag Day and Special Flag celebrations, see page 83 of this book.

THE STORY OF "OLD GLORY"

SINCE "the morning stars sang together and all the sons of God shouted for joy," there has never been such a glorious constellation as that in the deep blue sky of the American Flag. "Old Glory" has never known final defeat. Whenever war seemed to go against it for a while, it was only to teach us a needed lesson and strengthen our faith and love for our starry banner, and all that the Stars and Stripes stand for. In our dire need "they fought from Heaven," as ancient Deborah sang, "the stars in their courses fought against Sisera." Our "star of empire" can move "westward" no longer, so in future its way is onward and upward. During the troublous years of "wars and rumors of wars" there may have been a certain fitness in the accidental arrangement of the stars in straight rows, as if the very stars of heaven were marshalled according to the military manual, but now, in the Era of Peace, a true celestial constellation, the Flag of Peace, no longer a battle-flag, should lead the way to the highest triumphs of civilization.

Yet, with all our reverence for the Flag, every boy and girl must remember that the stars' future and ours are interwoven in the very bunting of each banner. If American men and women become slaves to habit, appetite and passion, our standard will no longer be "the Flag of the Frée." Cassius once said, according to Shakespeare,

> The fault, dear Brutus, is not in our *stars,*
> But in *ourselves,* that we are underlings.

What *is* an "underling"? Think of it! It is one who is "downed" by one little habit, which grows stronger and stronger while its victim gets weaker and weaker, till he says he "can't help it," and thus admits that he has become a little slave! When you know you are doing right you can "go ahead." "Thrice is he armed that hath his quarrel just." Our Flag has "never known defeat" because every man under it knew he was fighting for the right. "Conscience does make cowards of us all," Shakespeare puts into the mouth of Hamlet, when he had half a mind to commit suicide. If a boy does not want to be a coward he must keep his conscience bright and clean. One must not think things he would be ashamed to tell, for the things you *think* you will *be,* in spite of yourself! "As a man *thinketh,* so *is* he." But Emerson says that when a boy or man always tries his best to do the right thing, the very stars in heaven try to help him. So in real, earnest life, as in our national standard, we cut out the stars of our own destiny somewhat as Betsy Ross cut out the stars for the first Flag, and the "stars in their courses" reward us by fighting our battles. Every man or woman's greatest battle is with SELF, and the greatest victory is over SELF.

Let us return now to the visible banner made of bunting. Strange to relate, we did not weave our own bunting until after the Civil War! It was made abroad—in England, too!—and sent to us. But after that "cruel war was over," General Butler organized the United States Bunting Company of Lowell, Massachusetts, and the Government placed a duty of forty cent. on all imported buntings. As a result the American Navy Yards have used only American bunting since.

To describe the strange and wonderful flags that have been made would fill many volumes. Ambitious persons have put together "the largest Stars and Stripes ever made." One Flag may have been the biggest till a larger one was made. Then there have been wonderful banners made of all sorts of materials, from precious stones and electric lights to human beings. A number of "living flags" have been arranged along certain Presidential and Grand Army parades—in New Orleans, Portland (Oregon), St. Paul, Cleveland, and Seattle. The Portland children (dressed in red, white and blue, so seated on a grand stand as to look like the Stars and Stripes) went through a drill which made the great banner appear to wave in the breezes. The largest "living flag" of all was that in Cleveland, made up of twenty-five hundred children. The most interesting, perhaps, was that in Boston, during the Encampment of the Grand Army of the Republic, in August, 1904. The great flagstand was one hundred and twenty feet long and sixty feet wide, holding twenty-two hundred children. The stripes were rows of girls dressed in red, alternating with rows of girls in white. The canton was made up of "boys in blue," of whom forty-five held up forty-five white stars, the number of States in the Union then. (There are now 48 States, and 48 stars in our flag, since Oklahoma, New Mexico, and Arizona became States. The star of each new State is added with an appropriate ceremony on the next Fourth of July after the admission of that State to the Union.)   This human Flag was on the beautiful and historic Boston Common.   The children sang "The Star Spangled Banner," "Dixie," "My Maryland," "My Old Kentucky Home," and other patriotic songs, as the Grand Army marched past. It rained before the parade was over, but it is said that the *colors* of that loyal living Flag did not *"run!"*

It would be interesting to tell of the salutes to the Stars and Stripes, especially those of strange foreign princes and poten- tates. But that alone would make another vast volume.   For instance, we might describe the arrival of "His Royal High- ness S o m d e t c h Chowfa Maha Vah- jiravudh, the Crown Prince of Siam, and his brother, Prince Chakrabongse," in New York, October 10th, 1902.   But if you wish to read about such pageants as that, you will have to find "The Flag of the United States," a huge book of more than eight hundred pages, by Admiral P r e b l e, or "The Stars and Stripes and Other American Flags," by P. D. Harrison.   You are indebted to these two great flag au- thorities, as well as many smaller but e x c e l l e n t b o o k s, mostly written about Betsy Ross and her flag, f o r many of the facts w o v e n into *The Story of the Ameri-* *can Flag.*

HOLDING UP THE FLAG

Most of the States of the Union have passed laws forbidding the use of the Flag for advertising purposes, not allowing any lettering, even, to be printed on its sacred stripes.   This is a wise measure.   When General Grant was first nominated for the presidency, he saw, hanging over a street in Galena, Illinois, where he lived then, a campaign banner with "Grant and Colfax" lettered upon it.   He immediately asked that the Flag be taken down and the letter- ing removed, saying: "There is no name so great that it should be placed upon the Flag of our country."

The Flag on Independence Hall.

The American Flag Association was organized in New York City, in 1898, to use its influence to prevent the desecration of the Stars and Stripes. Many have suffered from the righteous wrath of those who saw or learned of their disrespect to the United States Flag. People suffering persecution and threatened with death in foreign lands have

INTERIOR OF INDEPENDENCE HALL

hailed the Star Spangled Banner with tears of joy and heart-breaking reverence, as did certain missionaries of Asiatic Turkey while the horrible massacres were going on there in 1909. Then "Old Glory" comes as the banner of love, light and salvation to the suffering and the dying.

How it got the name of "Old Glory" is an interesting story. Captain William Driver, of Salem, Massachusetts, was a ship-master who made around-the-world voyages. In 1831 he was captain of a brig named the *Charles Doggett*. Just as he was setting out on a voyage to the South Pacific Ocean, a party of friends brought him a large, beautifully made flag which Captain Driver sent up the mast at once. When it was unfurled and gracefully waving in the breeze above them, Captain Driver exclaimed in his ecstasy, *"Old Glory!"* This is the first time on record that our Flag was ever called "Old Glory."

The name must have made an impression, and the captain must have been in the habit of calling his Flag by that enthusiastic name, for he was known for many years as "Old Glory" Driver. During the Civil War he lived in Nashville, Tennessee, and for years "Old Glory" had to be kept hidden, but on a joyous day it was taken from its hiding-place to wave over the Tennessee State Capitol. "Old Glory" Driver gave his precious flag to his niece before he died, in 1882, after which she presented the original "Old Glory" to Essex Institute, in Salem, Massachusetts, the quaint old seaport where it first received the name which is now so familiar to us all.

THE FLAG IN WAR AND PEACE

HEN Abraham Lincoln was about to leave his home in Springfield, Illinois, to seize the broken helm of the Ship of State and try to steer her over the reefs and through the storms of civil war, a friend brought him a Flag with this inscription, in Hebrew, from the 5th and 9th verses of the first chapter of Joshua:

There shall not be any man able to stand before thee all the days of thy life; as I was with Moses, so will I be with thee; I will not fail thee nor forsake thee. . . . Have I not commanded thee? Be strong and of a good courage; be not afraid, neither be thou dismayed; for the Lord thy God is with thee whithersoever thou goest.

On his way to Washington, President-elect Lincoln arrived in Philadelphia on the 21st of February, 1861. As the next day was Washington's Birthday, he was asked to raise a new flag over Independence Hall in that city, where the Declaration of Independence was signed and where the Congress met that adopted the Stars and Stripes in the first place. In that ceremony Washington and Lincoln seemed to meet and shake hands with each other. In the little speech he made before pulling the flag up the staff he referred to the great principle of liberty, saying:

"If this country cannot be saved without giving up that principle, I was about to say I would rather be assassinated on this spot than surrender it."

ABRAHAM LINCOLN

Then the "halyards," or rope, was placed in his hands, and the beautiful banner went up to the top of the flagstaff. He afterward wrote that "it floated gloriously to the wind without an accident, in the bright, glowing sunshine of the morning."

President Lincoln's first great trouble was the firing on the Flag at Fort Sumter. During the bombardment the flagstaff was shot away. A soldier rushed out, and, at the risk of his life, caught it as it was falling,

nailed it to another staff and set it up again.   After a bombardment
of thirty-four hours, that brave little starving garrison was compelled
to leave the fort, which was burning on all sides.   The last thing they
did was to fire a round of fifty guns in honor of the dear old Flag.   The
men had taken their shirts off their backs to make the cartridges to
fire this final salute.   Then they lowered the Flag tenderly and took it
ashore with them.   This was on the 14th of April, 1861.   Some of the
men lived to see that Flag raised again, exactly four years afterwards,

BOMBARDMENT OF FORT SUMTER

on the 14th of April, 1865.   And Abraham Lincoln was assassinated
that very night—but the cruel war was over!   How everyone learned
to love and reverence the Stars and Stripes during that long and terrible war, from the time General Dix gave his famous order, before the
fighting began: *"If any man attempts to haul down the American Flag,
shoot him on the spot,"* to the day when all the soldiers who were living and able marched past the White House, in Washington, in the
Grand Review, and people shouted till they were hoarse, or wept with

sweet joy mingled with bitter sorrow, as the tattered Flags were car-ried past by those maimed and limping standard-bearers.

Then the Spanish War, a generation later, in 1898, brought all the people together in their demonstrations of affection for the old Flag. The North and the South were once more united in the war with Spain, and many of the heroes of that war, like Lieutenant Hobson and General Joe Wheeler, were gallant Southerners. Many of the young people of to-day can remember the great exultation over Dewey's victory at Manila Bay on May Day, that year, and of the tidings of the great rout of the Battle of Santiago that added to the joy of the celebration on that glorious Fourth of July, 1898. The same young

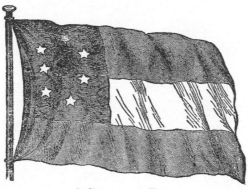

A CONFEDERATE FLAG

folks doubtless all remember about the freedom of Cuba, the adding of Porto Rico, the Hawaiian, Philippine and Samoan Islands, and little Guam, to the list of territories of the United States, where the "Flag of the Free" is floating over "the isles of the sea" where dusky people are learning to revere and love the Stars and Stripes, the banner of freedom and of civilization. For liberty follows Old Glory wherever it goes and the United States of America has now taken first rank as an acknowledged World Power.

If you want to learn how the Flag may be loved by one who has been denied even the right to look upon its lovely colors and folds, read "The Man without a Country," by Edward Everett Hale. If you can read

The Attack on Fort Sumter

that story without a lump in your throat and a tear in your eye, there is something the matter somewhere, unless you happen to be too young to appreciate the deep meaning of it. If so, read it again when you are a little older. You cannot read it too often.

It is the sincere belief of many men nowadays that enough blood has been shed already to make the dear old Flag as beautiful and as precious as it can possibly be. The great and enlightened nations are at last

BATTLE OF MANILA BAY

beginning to "learn war no more." The Czar of Russia has called for the founding of a Peace Tribunal, and Andrew Carnegie, "the grand old man of two worlds," is consecrating many millions of dollars to "peace on earth, good will toward men." Peace Day, May 18th, is already observed in our schools in commemoration of the first great Peace Convention at the Hague, in the Netherlands, in the interest of peace all around the world. The greatest men of the age are exerting their highest and best influence in behalf of universal peace. Theodore Roosevelt's taking of San Juan Hill was not so great an act as the bringing about of peace between Russia and Japan.

Solomon, the wise man, told us, long ago, that "He that ruleth his spirit is better than he that taketh a city." Our country will be what her men and women make her. It is a great thought that the future of our native land is in our own hands. If we are true and noble and loyal, America will continue to be what our fathers have made her, and what she is now known to be all the world over. It is a question of self-control, not whether we are "good shots" or not!

The United States of America has the highest mission in the world. She is yet to lead the way to the grandest achievement ever attempted by a World Power. She has taken her proper place in the forefront of the march of civilization. She is now "blazing a trail" for the whole world to follow. As the hosts of Israel saw before them, in the darkness, the pillar of fire and followed it, so that resplendent Banner of Peace (as it has been a standard of war)—the glorious Stars and Stripes, is now borne aloft to prove to all civilization that

Peace hath her victories
No less renowned than war.

A COLLECTION OF SONGS, POEMS, ADDRESSES, DRILLS, AND SAYINGS ABOUT THE STARS AND STRIPES

THE STAR-SPANGLED BANNER

FRANCIS SCOTT KEY, 1814

"Anacreon in Heaven"

SOLO OR QUARTET.

1. O say can you see, by the dawn's ear - ly light,
2. On the shore dim - ly seen thro' the mists of the deep,
3. And where is that band who so vaunt - ing - ly swore
4. O thus be it ev - er when free - men shall stand

What so proud - ly we hail'd at the twi - light's last gleam - ing?
Where the foe's haugh - ty host in dread si - lence re - pos - es,
That the hav - oc of war and the bat - tle's con - fu - sion,
Be - tween their lov'd home and wild war's des - o - la - tion;

Whose broad stripes and bright stars, thro' the per - il - ous fight,
What is that which the breeze, o'er the tow - er - ing steep,
A home and a coun - try should leave us no more?
Blest with vic - t'ry and peace, may the heav'n - res - cued land

O'er the ram - parts we watch'd, were so gal - lant - ly stream - ing?
As it fit - ful - ly blows, half con - ceals, half dis - clos - es?
Their blood has wash'd out their foul foot - steps' pol - lu - tion.
Praise the pow'r that hath made and pre - serv'd us a na - tion!

THE STAR-SPANGLED BANNER—Concluded

And the rock - ets' red glare, bombs burst - ing in air,
Now it catch - es the gleam of the morn - ing's first beam,
No ref - uge could save the hire - ling and slave
Then con - quer we must, when our cause it is just,

Gave proof thro' the night that our flag was still there.
In full glo - ry re - flect - ed, now shines on the stream:
From the ter - ror of flight or the gloom of the grave:
And this be our mot - to: "In God is our trust!"

CHORUS. ff

O say, does that star - span - gled ban - ner yet wave
'Tis the star - span - gled ban - ner: O, long may it wave
And the star - span - gled ban - ner in tri - umph doth wave
And the star - span - gled ban - ner in tri - umph doth wave

cres. ff

O'er the land of the free and the home of the brave?
O'er the land of the free and the home of the brave!
O'er the land of the free and the home of the brave.
O'er the land of the free and the home of the brave!

By permission of Ginn Publishing Co.

THE NATIONAL ENSIGN

ROBERT C. WINTHROP

Behold it! Listen to it! Every star has a tongue; every stripe is articulate. "There is no language or speech where their voices are not heard." There is magic in the web of it. It has an answer for every question of duty. It has a solution for every doubt and perplexity. It has a word of good cheer for every hour of gloom or of despondency.

Behold it! Listen to it! It speaks of earlier and of later struggles. It speaks of victories, and sometimes of reverses, on the sea and on the land. It speaks of patriots and heroes among the living and the dead. But before all and above all other associations and memories, whether of glorious men, or glorious deeds, or glorious places, its voice is ever of Union and Liberty, of the Constitution and the laws.

Behold it! Listen to it! Let it tell the story of its birth to these gallant volunteers, as they march beneath its folds by day, or repose beneath its sentinel stars by night! Let it recall to them the strange, eventful history of its rise and progress; let it rehearse to them the wonderful tale of its trials and triumphs, in peace as well as in war; and never let it be prostituted to any unworthy or unchristian purpose of revenge, depredation. or rapine!

THE NATIONAL FLAG

CHARLES SUMNER

There is the national Flag! He must be cold indeed who can look upon its folds rippling in the breeze without pride of country. If he be in a foreign land, the flag is companionship and country itself with all its endearments.

Who, as he sees it, can think of a state merely? Whose eyes, once fastened upon its radiant trophies, can fail to recognize the image of the whole nation?

It has been called a floating piece of poetry, and yet I know not if it have an intrinsic beauty beyond other ensigns. Its highest beauty is in what it symbolizes. It is because it represents all that all gaze at it with delight and reverence.

It is a piece of bunting lifted in the air, but it speaks sublimely, and every part has a voice. Its stripes of alternate red and white proclaim the original union of thirteen States to maintain the Declaration of Independence. Its stars of white on a field of blue proclaim that union of states constituting our national constellation, which receives a new star with every new state.

The two together signify union, past and present. The very colors have a language which was officially recognized by our fathers. White is for purity, red for valor, blue for justice; and all together, bunting, stripes, stars, and colors blazing in the sky, make the flag of our country—to be cherished by all our hearts, to be upheld by all our hands.

THE FLAG WOVEN OF HEROISM AND GRIEF
ALBERT J. BEVERIDGE

Do you remind me of the precious blood that must be shed, the lives that must be given, the broken hearts of loved ones for their slain? And this is indeed a heavier price than all combined. And yet as a Nation, every historic duty we have done, every achievement we have accomplished, has been by the sacrifice of our noblest sons. Every holy memory that glorifies the flag is of those heroes who died that its onward march might not be stayed. It is the Nation's dearest lives yielded for the flag that makes it dear to us; it is the Nation's most precious blood poured out for it that makes it precious to us. That flag is woven of heroism and grief, of the bravery of men, and women's tears, of righteousness and battle, of sacrifice and anguish, of triumph and glory. It is these which make our flag a holy thing. Who would tear from that sacred banner the glorious legends of a single battle where it has waved on land or sea? What son of a soldier of the flag whose father fell beneath it on any field would surrender that proud record for the heraldry of a king? In the cause of civilization, in the service of the Republic anywhere on earth, Americans consider wounds the noblest decorations man can win, and count the giving of their lives a glad and precious duty.

Pray God that spirit never fails. Pray God the time may never come when Mammon and the love of ease shall so debase our blood that we will fear to shed it for the flag and its imperial destiny. Pray God the time may never come when American heroism is but a legend like the story of the Cid, American faith in our mission and our might a dream dissolved, and the glory of our mighty race departed.

That time will never come. We will renew our youth at the fountain of new and glorious deeds. We will exalt our reverence for the flag by carrying it to a nobler future as well as by remembering its ineffable past. Its immortality will not pass, because everywhere and always we will acknowledge and discharge the solemn responsibilities our sacred flag, in its deepest meaning, puts upon us.

THE OLD FLAG RESTORED

PART OF HENRY WARD BEECHER'S ADDRESS AT THE RAISING OF THE UNION
FLAG OVER FORT SUMTER, APRIL 14, 1865

We raise our fathers' banner that it may bring back better blessings than those of old; that it may restore lawful government, and a prosperity purer and more enduring than that which it protected before; that it may win parted friends from their alienation; that it may inspire hope, and inaugurate universal liberty; that it may say to the sword, "Return to thy sheath," and to the plow and sickle, "Go forth;" that it may heal all jealousies, unite all policies, inspire a new national life, compact our strength, purify our principles, ennoble our national ambitions, and make this people great and strong, not for aggression and quarrelsomeness, but for the peace of the world, giving to us the glorious prerogative of leading all nations to juster laws, to more humane policies, to sincerer friendship, to rational, instituted civil liberty, and to universal Christian brotherhood.

Reverently, piously, in hopeful patriotism, we spread this banner on the sky, as of old the bow was planted on the cloud; and with solemn fervor beseech God to look upon it, and make it the memorial of an everlasting covenant and decree that never again on this fair land shall a deluge of blood prevail.

It was God Almighty who nailed our flag to the flagstaff, and I could not have lowered it if I had tried.

Major Robert Anderson.

THE OLD FLAG ABOVE ALL OTHERS
DAVID GREGG

Let no one run the red flag of anarchism over the Stars and Stripes, neither let anyone run the Stars and Stripes over the red flag. The two must never have any sort of union. Anarchism must not take the American republic under its protection, neither must the American republic take anarchism under its protection. We are living in a day when our country needs above all things intense Americans, who will Americanize every foreign thing, and will on no account allow America to be foreignized. Our fathers and brothers died for our country; it is our duty to live for it. We must pay a price as they paid a price. The price which we must pay for liberty is a pure manhood and an eternal vigilance. The monument which I would place by the graves of our noble dead would be, not a cold marble statue, but an honorable, wide-awake, honest, intelligent, moral, God-fearing American citizen.

My only defense is the flag of my country, and I place myself under its folds.

J. R. Poinsett.

I want no more honorable winding sheet than the brave old flag of the Union.

President Andrew Johnson.

If any man attempts to haul down the American flag, shoot him on the spot!

General John A. Dix.

One flag, one land, one heart, one hand,
One nation evermore.

O. W. Holmes.

We join ourselves to no party that does not carry the flag, and keep step to the music of the Union.

Rufus Choate.

THE FLAG FLOATS OVER AN UNDIVIDED LAND

J. M. CRAYETH

To-day the flag of our country floats over a land undivided, a Union saved, a government vindicated, a people free. As it waves above us in the calm atmosphere of peace, it seems transfigured by the mighty deeds that shed upon it unfading glory, and clothe it with an influence that shall one day loose the bands of despotism in other lands than ours, and open the gates of power throughout the world to the triumphant march of human freedom.

THE COST OF MAINTAINING THE FLAG

A. SHIRLEY LADD

The cost of maintaining the supremacy of the flag during the four years of 1861-1864 is partially shown by the following statistics:

The War of the Rebellion cost the United States, including all the expenses growing out of it, $6,189,929,908.58.

Total number of troops, regular and volunteer, enrolled for the Union was 2,859,132.

Number killed in battle, 61,362.

Died of wounds, 34,727.

Total number of lives given up in defense of the flag, "from which their blood has washed the black stain of slavery and made it the cleanest and brightest of all the national emblems of the earth," was 483,765.

No record could be made of the sorrow and anguish of the wives, mothers, sisters, and sweethearts of those who went to the front, or of the sufferings and hardships endured by the "Boys in Blue."

THE MAINTENANCE OF THE FLAG DUE TO THE SOLDIERS' BRAVERY

MAJOR J. B. THOMAS

The flag that floats above us, whose every fold is suggestive of the noble actions of those whom we now honor, whose every star is only one more gem saved to adorn these shrines, whose every rustling breeze, the security their sacrifices have rendered to it, are all combined to make the memory of this day a treasure to be cherished, honored, and revered.

THE AMERICAN FLAG WITHOUT A RIVAL

J. C. J. LANGBIEN

In all the world there is not such another flag, that carries within its ample folds such grandeur of hope, as our dear old American flag, made by and for liberty, nourished in its spirit, and carried in its service; its priceless value cannot be estimated; wherever our flag has gone it has been the herald of a better day; it has been the pledge of freedom, justice, order, civilization, and of Christianity.

THE BATTLE-FLAGS PROCLAIM UNION ONLY

CARL SCHURZ

Let the battle-flag of our brave volunteers which they brought home from the war, with the glorious record of their victories, be preserved as a proud ornament in our State houses and armories—but let the colors of the army under which the sons of all the States are to meet and mingle in common patriotism speak of nothing but union.

THE SCHOOLS TAKE PART

COLONEL HENRY WATTERSON

In every part of the American Union, the children are taking up the wondrous tale of the discovery of America by Christopher Columbus, and from Boston to Galveston, from the little log school-house in the wilderness to the towering academy in the city or town, may be witnessed by the unprecedented spectacle of a powerful nation captured by an army of Lilliputians, of embryo men and women, to toddling boys and girls, and tiny elves, scarce big enough to lisp the numbers of the National Anthem, scarce strong enough to lift the miniature flags that make of arid street and autumn wood an emblematical garden, to gladden the sight and to glorify the Red, White and Blue. . . .

These, indeed, are our crown-jewels, the truest, though the inevitable offspring of our civil development; the representatives of a manhood vitalized and invigorated by toil and care, of a womanhood elated and inspired by Liberty and Education.

God bless the children and their mothers! God bless our country's flag, and God be with us now and ever! God in the roof-trees' shade, and God in the highway! God in the wind and the waves! God in all our hearts!

This flag is an emblem to represent the birth of a free nation.

Mrs. Elizabeth ("Betsy") Ross.

The American flag must wave over States, not over Provinces.

Rutherford B. Hayes.

CEREMONY OF RAISING THE FLAG OVER THE PUBLIC SCHOOL

FLAG DAY, JUNE 14TH

First Arranged by *The Youth's Companion*

LETTER OF PRESENTATION
ADDRESS OF ACCEPTANCE
DECLAMATION, "The National Flag"......Charles Sumner (Page 86)
READING OF POEM, "Our Colors".......Laura E. Richards (Page 100)
SINGING, "The Star Spangled Banner"..Francis Scott Key (Page 84)
RAISING THE FLAG
THREE CHEERS FOR THE FLAG!
SINGING, "Flag of the Free"...........................(Page 101)
ADDRESS, "Patriotism in the Public School"
SINGING, "America"..................................(Page 93)

This program is, of course, only suggestive. Teachers and friends of the school can easily add other selections and features. Those to make the address of acceptance and the address on "Patriotism in the Public Schools" can be selected from local speakers.

AMERICA

S. F. SMITH.

Adapted by HENRY CAREY.

1. My coun - try! 'tis of thee, Sweet land of lib - er - ty,
2. My na - tive coun - try, thee, Land of the no - ble free—
3. Let mu - sic swell the breeze, And ring from all the trees
4. Our fa - ther's God! to Thee, Au - thor of lib - er - ty,

Of thee I sing, Land where my fa - thers died! Land of the
Thy name I love, I love thy rocks and rills, Thy woods and
Sweet free - dom's song: Let mor - tal tongues a - wake; Let all that
To Thee we sing: Long may our land be bright With free - dom's

Pil - grim's pride! From ev - 'ry moun - tain side Let free - dom ring!
tem - pled hills: My heart with rap - ture thrills Like that a - bove.
breathe par - take; Let rocks their si - lence break,— The sound pro - long.
ho - ly light; Pro - tect us by Thy might, Great God, our King!

5 I love thine inland seas,
  Thy groves of giant trees,
    Thy rolling plains;
  Thy rivers' mighty sweep,
  Thy mystic canyons deep,
  Thy mountains wild and steep,
    All thy domains;

6 Thy silver Eastern strands
  Thy Garden Gate that stands
    Wide to the West
  Thy flowery Southland fair,
  Thy sweet and crystal air,—
  O land beyond compare,
    Thee I love best.

By permission of Ginn Publishing Co.

A NEW FLAG DRILL

FROM "FLAG DAY IN THE SCHOOLROOM"

(In this drill the hands are used alternately. Each child has only one flag. The fatigue is less than in a two-handed exercise, and at the same time attention to the leader and prompt movement are cultivated by the necessity of changing flags at a certain note of the music, as there is no pause in the drill for changes. Independent movement of the left hand is also gained. The prettiest effect is produced by using single flags made of a bright-colored sateen, attached to strong bamboo canes about eighteen inches long. The canes are easy to handle, and the soft sateen flags flutter and wave in the air with much better effect than the stiff paper flags sometimes used.)

PASSING DRILL

As the children stand in rows facing the teacher, the child at end of each row (on the teacher's left) should have a bundle of flags handed to him, corresponding in number with the children in the row. (The rows should be well apart, but the children should be within easy reaching distance of each other.) The end child should hold the bundle of flags in his right hand, take one with his left, and hold it straight out, with his elbow to his side. The orders for passing are:

"*One: Right hand on flags.*" When the second child in each row places his right hand on the flagstick which the first child is holding, just in front of the first child's hand.

"*Two: Flags up.*" When the second child in each row suddenly holds up the flag he grasped at "One," while the first child looses it and gets another in position.

"*Three: Down and change.*" When the second child brings his flag down smartly into his left hand and holds it out ready for the third child to place his hand upon.

At the second repetition of "One" the second child places his hand on the first child's flag, and the third child places his on the second child's. When "Two" is repeated, the second and third children hold up the flags they had previously grasped in their right hands. When

"Three" is repeated, the second and third children bring down flags into left hands. And so, at each repetition of the passing orders, one child more gets a flag, until all the flags are passed along the row. When the children are familiar with the orders, they should pass to "One," "Two," "Three,' repeated slowly and then pretty quickly, and finally should pass to music rather slowly played, or sung by themselves. If thirteen stand in a row, twelve bars of three-quarter time, played in moderate time, should be furnished at the last movement. The children now stand, each with a flag held out in the left hand.

The teacher says, "Position!" and each child passes his flag back into his right hand, with right elbow to side, left hand hanging down, heels together and head erect. A patriotic song should be sung before the drill is continued.

FIRST EXERCISE

("The Blue Bells of Scotland" may be played for the following movements:)

To the first four bars of four-quarter music make eight movements, making the first on the second note of the tune, so as to start with a strong accent. Begin with flags in "Position 1."

(1) Hold up flags quickly, as high as possible, with elbows straightened.

(2) Lower suddenly to "Position 1."

(3) and (4) Same as (1) and (2).

(5) and (6) Same as (1) and (2).

(7) Same as (1).

(8) Pass flags into left hands and hold at "Position 1."

To the next four bars of the music repeat the same exercise with left hands, returning flags to right hands at 8 and hold *out* with elbow to side. To the next four bars of music stretch out right arms to full extent for 1, draw back elbows to sides for 2. Repeat, and change flags to same position in left hands at 8. To next four bars of music repeat the same exercise with left hands, returning flags to right hands in "Position 1" at 8.

FLAG PLAY

FOR PRIMARY CHILDREN—FROM "FLAG DAY IN THE SCHOOLROOM"

(1) Pretty bright flags have we,
Waving on (2) *high;*
  (3)*Up* they go, (4) *down* they go.
Now they are (5) *nigh;*
  Now they are (6) *far away,*
Now they are (7) *nigh;*
  Now they point (8) *upwards,*
To skies bright and clear.
  (9) *Under* and (10) *over,* so
(11) *Above* and (12) *below,*
  (13) *Backwards* and (14) *forwards*
  Our flags they go.
  We've (15) *red, blue,* and *yellow,*
  Some pretty *green* too.
(16) If you will look at us
We'll show them to you.
  Hurrah for our play time!
We babies like fun.
  And yet we are sorry
When lessons are done.

MOTIONS

1. Flags held up.
2. Wave above head.
3. Raise arm above head.
4. Let arm drop and point flag to floor.
5. Bring flag in front near body.
6 Stretch out arm in front at right angles to body.
7. Bring in front again near body, and show that "nigh" and "near" have the same meaning.

8. Stretch far above head.
9. Under chin.
10. Over head.
11. Left hand held in front, flag placed above hand.
12. Flag placed below hand.
13, 14. Flags brought smartly in front of body, then behind, then forwards and backwards alternately. Questions as to why they cannot see flags when they sway backwards (position of eyes).

By permission of the Penn Publishing Company.

THE FLAG GOES BY

HENRY HOLCOMB BENNETT

Hats off!
Along the street there comes
A blare of bugles, a ruffle of drums,
A flash of color beneath the sky:
        Hats off!
The Flag is passing by!

Blue and crimson and white it shines,
Over the steel-tipped, ordered lines.
        Hats off!
The Colors before us fly;
But more than the Flag is passing by.

Sea-fights and land-fights, grim and great,
Fought to make and to save the state;
Weary marches, and sinking ships;
Cheers of victory on dying lips;

Days of plenty, and years of peace;
March of a strong land's swift increase;
Equal justice, right and law,
Stately honor and reverend awe;

Sign of a nation, great and strong
To ward her people from foreign wrong;
Pride and glory and honor, all
Live in the Colors to stand or fall.

Hats off!
Along the street there comes
A blare of bugles, a ruffle of drums;
And loyal hearts are beating high;
Hats off!
The Flag is passing by!

This is an inspiring and patriotic poem for Arbor Day and other occasions. It should be recited with spirit.

Many teachers instruct their pupils to remove their hats when the Flag passes by. This is a most beautiful and patriotic custom. Respect for the Flag cannot be taught too early.

TWO SOUTHERN TOASTS

At a reunion of Southern Veterans of the Mexican and Civil Wars, the following toast was given to the Stars and Stripes:

"Under this flag we once fought and
It was victorious,
Against this flag we once fought and
It was victorious;
Again it is our flag; may it ever
Be victorious."

VERSES FOR A SMALL BOY TO SPEAK AT FLAG RAISING

F. H. S.

From "Our Holidays," Arranged by Matilda Blair.

I'm not so old as some I see,
    But long ago I knew
The finest colors in the world
    Were red and white and blue.

The red is in our rosy cheeks,
    And in our eyes the blue,
The white is in our hearts when they
    Are honest, pure and true.

The deepest blue of all the sky,
    The red of sunset hours,
The white, from softest fleecy clouds,
    Meet in this flag of ours.

And as its colors are of Heaven,
    We will believe that He
Whose hand upholds the universe
    Will guard our colors three.

Then fling it wide upon the breeze,
    With loyal hearts and true,
Hurrah for great America,
    The Red, the White, the Blue!

By permission of McLoughlin Brothers.

7—*The Story of the American Flag.*

OUR COLORS

LAURA E. RICHARDS

RED! 'tis the hue of the battle,
    The pledge of victory;
    In sunset light, in northern night,
    It flashes brave and free.
    "Then paint with red thy banner,"
    Quoth Freedom to the land,
    "And when thy sons go forth to war,
    This sign be in their hand."

WHITE! 'tis the sign of purity,
    Of everlasting truth;
    The snowy robe of childhood,
    The stainless mail of youth.
    Then paint with white thy banner,
    And pure as northern snow
    May these thy stately children
    In truth and honor go.

BLUE! 'tis the tint of heaven,
    The morning's gold-shot arch,
    The burning deeps of noontide,
    The stars' unending march.
    Then paint with blue thy banner,
    And bid thy children raise
    At daybreak, noon and eventide
    Their hymn of love and praise.

VALOR and TRUTH and RIGHTEOUSNESS,
    In threefold strength to-day,
    Raise high the flag triumphant,
    The banner glad and gay.
    "And keep thou well thy colors,"
    Quoth Freedom to the land,
    "And 'gainst a world of evil
    Thy sons and thou shall stand."

By permission of *The Youth's Companion*.

FLAG OF THE FREE

Steady time.

From "Lohengrin"

1. Flag of the free, fair - est to see! Borne thro' the strife and the
2. Flag of the brave! long may it wave, Cho - sen of God while His

thun - der of war; Ban - ner so bright with star - ry light,
might we a - dore, In Lib - er - ty's van for man - hood of man,

D. S.—While thro' the sky loud rings the cry,

Float ev - er proud - ly from moun-tain to shore. Em - blem of Free - dom,
Sym - bol of Right thro' the years pass-ing o'er! Pride of our coun - try,

FINE.

Un - ion and Lib - er - ty! One ev - er - more!

D. S.

hope to the slave, Spread thy fair folds but to shield and to save,
hon - ored a - far, Scat - ter each cloud that would dark - en a star,

By permission of Ginn Publishing Co.

"I'M FOR THAT FLAG FOREVER!"

FRANK L. STANTON.

But now I'm in the Union. I see there, overhead,
The flag our fathers fought for; her rippling rills of red

All glorious and victorious; the splendor of her stars—
And I say: "The blood of heroes dyed all her crimson bars."

I'm for that flag forever, 'gainst foes on sea and shore;
Who shames her? Who defames her? Give me my gun once more.

We'll answer when they need us—when the war-fires light the night;
There's a Lee still left to lead us to the glory of the fight.

We're one in heart forever—we're one in heart and hand;
The flag's a challenge to the sea, a garland on the land;

We're united—one great country; freedom's the watchword still,
There's a Lee that's left to lead us—let the storm break where it will.

———————

For every star in its field of blue,
For every stripe of stainless hue,
Ten thousand of the tried and true
Have laid them down and died.

FLAG OF THE HEROES

OLIVER WENDELL HOLMES.

Flag of the heroes who left us their glory,
   Borne through their battlefields' thunder and flame,
Blazoned in song and illumined in story,
   Wave o'er us all who inherit their fame!
     Up with our banner bright,
     Sprinkled with starry light,
Spread its fair emblems from mountain to shore,
     While through the sounding sky
     Loud rings the Nation's cry,—
UNION AND LIBERTY! ONE EVERMORE!

By permission of Houghton, Mifflin & Co.

RAISE HIGH THE FLAG TRIUMPHANT

THE FLAG ABOVE THE SCHOOL-HOUSE DOOR

HARRIET CROCKER LE ROY

In cities and in villages, in country districts scattered wide,
Above the school-house door it floats—a thing of beauty and of pride;
The poorest child, the richest heir—'tis theirs in common to adore,
For 'tis *their* flag that proudly floats—the flag above the school-house
    door!

What does it mean, O careless boy, O thoughtless girl, at happy play?
Red for the blood your fathers shed on some far off eventful day—
White for the loyalty and faith of countless women who forbore
To mourn, but gave their all to save the flag above the school-house door,

And blue—sweet hope's ethereal hue—the color of true loyalty—
Red, white and blue, united in one grand, harmonious trinity!
'Tis yours to love! 'tis yours to serve! 'tis yours to cherish evermore!
God keep it ever floating there—the flag above the school-house door!

By permission of *The Youth's Companion.*

THE FLAG IN NATURE

SAMUEL H. SMITH.

All nature sings wildly the song of the free,
The red, white and blue floats o'er land and o'er sea:
The white in each billow that breaks on the shore,
The blue in the arching that canopies o'er
The land of our birth, in its glory outspread—
Day fades into night, and the red stripes retire,
But stars o'er the blue light their sentinel fires,
And though night be gloomy with clouds overspread,
Each star holds its place in the field overhead;
When scatter the clouds and the tempest is through,
We count every star in the field of the blue.

OUR FLAG IS THERE

WRITTEN BY AN AMERICAN NAVAL OFFICER, 1812.

Our flag is there, our flag is there!
  We'll hail it with three loud huzzas;
Our flag is there, our flag is there,
  Behold the glorious Stripes and Stars.
Stout hearts have fought for that bright flag,
  Strong hands sustained it mast-head high,
And, oh, to see how proud it waves,
  Brings tears of joy in every eye.

That flag has stood the battle's roar,
  With foeman stout, with foeman brave;
Strong hands have sought that flag to lower,
  And found a speedy watery grave.
That flag is known on every shore,
  The standard of a gallant band;
Alike unstained in peace or war,
  It floats o'er Freedom's happy land.

A FLAG FOR THE SCHOOL-HOUSE

FROM "FLAG DAY IN THE SCHOOLROOM"

From every school-house in the land
  Let the hallowed flag of Union wave
And float aloft on every breeze,
  Above the heads of children brave.
Unite around that dear old flag,
  From Eastern strand to Western shore,
From Northern bound to Southern gulf,
  The hearts of children evermore.

Inspire Columbia's joyful youth
  With fervent love of country grand;
That when they reach life's proud estate
  They'll nobly by our Nation stand,
And guard her safe from ev'ry foe
  Of equal rights and freedom's cause,
And keep for aye inviolate
  Her constitution and her laws.

Yes, hoist the starry banner up,
  Emblem of our country's glory,
And teach the children of our land
  Its grand and wondrous story,
Of how in early times it waved
  High o'er the Continentals brave
Who fought and made this country free,
  The one true home of liberty.

By permission of the Penn Publishing Company, Philadelphia.

THE OLD FLAG FOREVER

FRANK L. STANTON.

She's up there—Old Glory—where lightnings are sped;
She dazzles the nations with ripples of red;
And she'll wave for us living, or droop o'er us dead—
The flag of our country forever!

She's up there—Old Glory—how bright the stars stream!
And the stripes like red signals of liberty gleam!
And we dare for her, living, or dream the last dream
'Neath the flag of our country forever!

She's up there—Old Glory—no tyrant-dealt scars
Nor blur on her brightness, no stain on her stars!
The bright blood of heroes hath crimsoned her bars—
She's the flag of our country forever!

THE FLAG

ARTHUR MACY

Here comes The Flag!
Hail it!
Who dares to drag
Or trail it?
Give it hurrahs,—
Three for the stars,
Three for the bars.
Uncover your head to it!
The soldiers who tread to it
Shout at the sight of it,
The justice and right of it,
The unsullied white of it,
The blue and the red of it,
And tyranny's dread of it!

Here comes The Flag!
Cheer it!
Valley and crag
Shall hear it.
Fathers shall bless it,
Children caress it.
All shall maintain it,
No one shall stain it.
Cheers for the sailors that fought on the wave for it,
Cheers for the soldiers that always were brave for it,
Tears for the men that went down to the grave for it.
Here comes The Flag!

By permission of *The Youth's Companion.*

BARBARA FRIETCHIE

JOHN GREENLEAF WHITTIER.

Up from the meadows rich with corn,
Clear in the cool September morn,
The clustered spires of Frederick stand
Green-walled by the hills of Maryland.
Round about them orchards sweep,
Apple and peach tree, fruited deep,
Fair as the garden of the Lord
To the eyes of the famished rebel horde,
On that pleasant morn of the early fall
When Lee marched over the mountain wall;
Over the mountains winding down,
Horse and foot, into Frederick town.

Forty flags with their silver stars,
Forty flags with their crimson bars,
Flapped in the morning wind; the sun
Of noon looked down, and saw not one.
Up rose old Barbara Frietchie then,
Bowed with her four score years and ten;
Bravest of all in Frederick town,
She took up the flag the men hauled down;
In her attic window the staff she set,
To show that one heart was loyal yet.

Up the street came the rebel tread,
Stonewall Jackson riding ahead.
Under his slouched hat left and right
He glanced; the old flag met his sight,
"Halt!"—the dust-brown ranks stood fast.
"Fire!"—out blazed the rifle-blast.
It shivered the window, pane and sash;

BARBARA FRIETCHIE AND THE FLAG

It rent the banner with seam and gash.
Quick, as it fell from the broken staff,
Dame Barbara snatched the silken scarf;
She leaned far out on the window-sill,
And shook it forth with a royal will.
"Shoot, if you must, this old gray head,
But spare your country's flag," she said.

A shade of sadness, a blush of shame,
Over the face of the leader came;
The nobler nature within him stirred
To life at that woman's deed and word;
"Who touches a hair of yon gray head
Dies like a dog! March on!" he said.

All day long through Frederick street
Sounded the tread of marching feet;
All day long that free flag tossed
Over the heads of the rebel host.
Ever its torn folds rose and fell
On the loyal winds that loved it well;
And through the hill-gaps sunset light
Shone over it with a warm good night.

Barbara Frietchie's work is o'er,
And the rebel rides on his raids no more.
Honor to her! and let a tear
Fall, for her sake, on Stonewall's bier.
Over Barbara Frietchie's grave,
Flag of Freedom and Union, wave!
Peace and order and beauty draw
Round thy symbol of light and law;
And ever the stars above look down
On thy stars below in Frederick town!

By permission of Houghton, Mifflin & Co.

FREEDOM'S FLAG

JOHN J. HOOD.

Our country's flag! O emblem dear
  Of all the soul loves best,
What glories in thy folds appear
  Let noble deeds attest:
Thy presence on the field of strife
  Enkindles valor's flame;
Around thee in the hour of peace,
  We twine our nation's fame.

CHORUS.

Then hurrah, hurrah, for Freedom's Flag!
  We hail with ringing cheers,
Its glowing bars and clust'ring stars,
  That have braved a hundred years.

Beneath thy rays our fathers bled
  In freedom's holy cause;
Where'er to Heaven thy folds outspread,
  Prevail sweet Freedom's laws.
Prosperity has marked thy course
  O'er all the land and sea;
Thy favored sons in distant climes,
  Still fondly look to thee.—*Chorus.*

Proud banner of the noble free!
  Emblazon'd from on high!
Long may thy folds unsoil'd reflect
  The glories of the sky!
Long may thy land be Freedom's land,
  Thy homes with virtue bright,
Thy sons a brave united band,
  For God, for Truth, and right!—*Chorus.*

THE STARS AND STRIPES

Arr.

1. O Star - span - gled ban - ner! O red, white, and blue!
2. In - vin - ci - ble ban - ner! the flag of the free!
3. O God of our fa - thers! this ban - ner must shine

The hearts of all free - men turn fond - ly to you;
O where treads the foot that would fal - ter for thee?
Where bat - tle is hot - test, in ware - fare di - vine.

And strong arms are read - y to strike with a will
Give tears for the part - ing— a mur - mur ot pray'r—
O lead us, till wide from the Gulf to the sea,

Till foes of our free - dom are hum - bled and still.
Then, for - ward! the fame of our stand - ard to share.
The land shall be sa - cred to free - dom and Thee.

SONG OF THE FLAG

HEZEKIAH BUTTERWORTH

Cheer, cheer we the Flag of the nation,
  On liberty's breeze unfurled,
The glory of manhood's creation,
  The Pilot of Peace in the world.
Cheer the Flag that our fathers, undaunted,
  Proclaimed, when the nation was new,
Should float for the freedom they planted,
  And be to the Right ever true.

CHORUS.

  Cheer, cheer we the Flag ever true!
  Cheer, cheer we the Flag ever true!
  The Flag by the patriots planted,
  The Flag to the Right ever true.

Flag that floats for that morning of wonder
  That heard on the ocean impearled
The gun of the caravel thunder
  That shook the new shores of the world;
Flag that floats in its majesty splendid,
  And shall float in humanity's name,
For the cause that our fathers defended,
  For the Right on the red fields of flame.—*Chorus.*

Old banners of royalty faded,
  The lions, the lilies of gold,
And the Flag no dishonor had shaded,
  The stars of the empire enrolled,
And bore it, the pioneers glorious,
  The dim forest-ways as they trod,
From ocean to ocean victorious,
  For the Right and the freedom of God.—*Chorus.*

Let the School, for America's glory,
 The pledge of the fathers renew;
Four hundred years thrilling with story,
 A thousand years rising in view;
And as long as the old constellation
 Shall gleam on the Flag of the light,
The School shall be true to the Nation,
 And the Nation be true to the Right.

By permission of *The Youth's Companion.*

THE YOUNG PATRIOTS' SONG

ELIZABETH LLOYD

Tune, "Marching Through Georgia."

We're the future citizens, now sing an earnest song,
Sing it with a purpose that befits the true and strong,
Sing it with a spirit that will help the world along,
 For we are growing and striving.

CHORUS.

Hurrah! Hurrah! Our own Red, White, and Blue!
Hurrah! Hurrah! We're loyal, brave, and true!
For our country and her banner bright our best we'll ever do,
 While we are growing and striving.

Little lessons daily learned will make us truly wise;
Little duties bravely done will win the hero's prize;
Up the hill of earnest toil the road to honor lies,
 And we are growing and striving.—*Chorus.*

Here we pledge allegiance to our own dear native land,
For the service of the State we train the head and hand,
Only noble citizens can make a Nation grand,
 So we are growing and striving.—*Chorus.*

OLD FLAG

HUBBARD PARKER

What shall I say to you, Old Flag?
You are so grand in every fold,
So linked with mighty deeds of old,
So steeped in blood where heroes fell,
So torn and pierced by shot and shell,
So calm, so still, so firm, so true,
My throat swells at the sight of you,
       Old Flag!

What of the men who lifted you, Old Flag,
Upon the top of Bunker Hill,
Who crushed the Briton's cruel will,
'Mid shock and roar and crash and scream,
Who crossed the Delaware's frozen stream,
Who starved, who fought, who bled, who died,
That you might float in glorious pride,
       Old Flag?

What of the women brave and true, Old Flag,
Who, while the cannon thundered wild,
Sent forth a husband, lover, child,
Who labored in the field by day,
Who, all the night long, knelt to pray,
And thought that God great mercy gave,
If only freely you might wave,
       Old Flag?

What is your mission now, Old Flag?
What but to set all people free,
To rid the world of misery,
To guard the right, avenge the wrong,
And gather in one joyful throng
Beneath your folds in close embrace
All burdened ones of every race,
       Old Flag.

8—*The Story of the American Flag.*

GOD SAVE THE FLAG

OLIVER WENDELL HOLMES.

Washed in the blood of the brave and the blooming,
   Snatched from the altars of insolent foes,
Burning with star-fires, but never consuming,
   Flash its broad ribbons of lily and rose.

Vainly the prophets of Baal would rend it,
   Vainly its worshipers pray for its fall;
Thousands have died for it, millions defend it,
   Emblem of justice and mercy to all:

Justice that reddens the sky with her terrors,
   Mercy that comes with her white-handed train,
Soothing all passions, redeeming all errors,
   Sheathing the sabre and breaking the chain.

Borne on the deluge of old usurpations,
   Drifted our Ark o'er the desolate seas,
Bearing the rainbow of hope to the nations,
   Torn from the storm-cloud and flung to the breeze!

God bless the Flag and its loyal defenders ,
   While its broad folds o'er the battlefield wave,
Till the dim star-wreath rekindle its splendors,
   Washed from its stains in the blood of the brave!

By permission of Houghton, Mifflin & Co.

THE FLOWER OF LIBERTY

OLIVER WENDELL HOLMES

What flower is this that greets the morn,
Its hues from Heaven so freshly born?
With burning star and flaming band
It kindles all the sunset land:
Oh, tell us what its name may be,—
Is this the Flower of Liberty?
    It is the banner of the free,
    The starry Flower of Liberty!

In savage Nature's far abode
Its tender seed our fathers sowed;
The storm-winds rocked its swelling bud,
Its opening leaves were streaked with blood
Till lo! earth's tyrants shook to see
The full-blown Flower of Liberty!
    Then hail the banner of the free,
    The starry Flower of Liberty!

Behold its streaming rays unite,
One mingling flood of braided light,—
The red that fires the Southern rose,
With spotless white from Northern snows,
And, spangled o'er its azure, see
The sister Stars of Liberty!
    Then hail the banner of the free,
    The starry Flower of Liberty!

The blades of heroes fence it round,
Where'er it springs is holy ground,
From tower and dome its glories spread;
It waves where lonely sentries tread;
It makes the land as ocean free,
And plants an empire on the sea!
    Then hail the banner of the free,
    The starry Flower of Liberty!

  Thy sacred leaves, fair Freedom's flower,
  Shall ever float on dome and tower,
  To all their heavenly colors true,
  In blackening frost or crimson dew,—
  And God love us as we love thee,
  Thrice holy Flower of Liberty!
    Then hail the banner of the free,
    The starry Flower of Liberty!

By permission of Houghton, Mifflin & Co.

STAND BY THE FLAG

JOHN NICHOLAS WILDER

Stand by the Flag! Its stars, like meteors gleaming,
 Have lighted Arctic icebergs, southern seas,
And shone responsive to the stormy beaming
 Of old Arcturus and the Pleiades.

Stand by the Flag! Its stripes have streamed in glory,
 To foes a fear, to friends a festal robe,
And spread in rhythmic lines the sacred story
 Of freedom's triumphs over all the globe.

Stand by the Flag! On land and ocean billow
 By it your fathers stood unmoved and true,
Living, defended; dying, from their pillow,
 With their last blessing, passed it on to you.

Stand by the Flag! Immortal heroes bore it
 Through sulphurous smoke, deep moat and armed defense;
And their imperial Shades still hover o'er it,
 A guard celestial from Omnipotence.

A FREE LAND AND A FREE FLAG

I see a room with faces bright,
    And eyes that sparkle clear,
And children sing the songs they love
    Of home and country dear.

For little children love to hear
    Of those men strong and brave,
Who worked and fought and died for us,
    Who did our country save.

Once these same men we talk of now
    Were just as small as we,
They learned to love this flag of ours,
    Which waves o'er all the free.

And if we love it when we're small
    And those who made it grand,
When we get old enough to vote
    We'll keep this a free land.

COMRADES! JOIN THE FLAG OF GLORY

In 1813, by an Unknown Writer

Comrades! join the flag of glory,
    Cheerily tread the deck of fame,
Earn a place in future story,
    Seek and win a warrior's name.

Yankee tars can laugh at dangers,
    While the roaring mountain wave
Teems with carnage—they are strangers
    To a deed that is not brave.

May our bannered stars as ever
    Splendidly o'er freeman burn,
Till the night of war is over,
    Till the dawn of peace return.

THE BANNER OF THE STARS

R. W. RAYMOND

Hurrah! boys, hurrah! fling our banner to the breeze!
Let the enemies of freedom see its folds again unfurled.
And down with the pirates that scorn upon the seas
Our victorious Yankee banner, sign of Freedom to the World!

CHORUS.

We'll never have a new flag, for ours is the true flag,
The true flag, the true flag, the Red, White and Blue flag,
Hurrah! boys, hurrah! we will carry to the wars
The old flag, the free flag, the banner of the Stars.

And what tho' its white shall be crimsoned with our blood?
And what tho' its stripes shall be shredded in the storms?
To the torn flag, the worn flag, we'll keep our promise good,
And we'll bear the starry blue field, with gallant hearts and arms.
—*Chorus.*

Then, cursed be he who would strike our starry flag!
May the God of hosts be with us, as we smite the traitor down!
And cursed be he who would hesitate or lag,
Till the dear flag, the fair flag, with Victory we crown.—*Chorus.*

THE LANGUAGE OF THE FLAG

CAMDEN M. COBERN

The Star Spangled Banner of Freedom was always beautiful, but
never as beautiful as now. The very colors have a language known
and read of all men. The groundwork of the flag, as of the Union, is
whitenesss, white being the symbol of truthfulness, righteousness, and
purity, and drawn across that white face—white as an angel's wing—
is the crimson band which from creation's morning has symbolized all

the courage and self-sacrifice and open-veined manhood which can flow in wide streams from the gaping wounds of patriot and hero. And pressed close upon that seamless robe of purity, and close beside the costly crimson streams that flow like rivers of salvation over it is the blue of heaven for clearness, out of which shine the mysterious, deathless stars, lighting the night with cheerful fires.

Ah, yes, the blue of the ocean and of the sky is there, and on whatever coast the deep blue ocean beats, and over whatever people the peaceful firmament bends down like God's own pity, the starry flag shall shed its triumphant, beneficent, celestial influence. The stars and all the powers of heaven are there, and so surely as the stars in their courses fought against Sisera in the olden time, so will they fight now for the flag which is the emblem of righteousness, and truth, and freedom.

KEEP OUR BANNER SPOTLESS!

Ah! what a mighty trust is ours, the noblest ever sung,
To keep this banner spotless its kindred stars among!
Our fleets may throng the ocean—our forts the headlands crown—
Our mines their treasure lavish for mint and mart and town.
Rich fields and flocks and busy looms bring plenty, far and wide—
And statelier temples deck the land than Rome's or Athens' pride—
And science dare the mysteries of earth and wave and sky—
Till none with us in splendor and strength and skill can vie;
Yet, should we reckon Liberty and Manhood less than these,
And slight the right of the humblest between our circling seas,—
Should we be false to our sacred past, our fathers' God forgetting,
This banner would lose its lustre, our sun be nigh his setting!
But the dawn will sooner forget the east, the tides their ebb and flow,
Than you forget our radiant flag, and its matchless gifts forego!
Nay! you will keep it high-advanced with ever-brightening sway—
The banner whose light betokens the Lord's diviner day
Leading the nations gloriously in Freedom's holy way!
No cloud on the field of azure—no stain on the rosy bars—
God bless you, Youth and Maidens, as you guard the Stripes and Stars!

By permission of *The Youth's Companion.*

THE OLD THIRTEEN

July 4, 1901.

THERON BROWN

Blue tides of a hundred harbor bays
　　That kiss the capes of a thousand miles,
Sing joy for Liberty's Day of days,
　　And mantle your surf in golden smiles!
From green Savannah to Portsmouth Sound
　　Your seaboard sand is her glory land,
Where the sunrise shore of her realm she found,
　　And cradled a hemisphere in her hand,
And Plymouth and Jamestown crowned her queen
In the deathless league of the Old Thirteen.

'Tis the day of trumpet and cannon blast,
　　Of blazing rocket and rolling drum,
For the hundred years of a splendid past
　　And a grander hundred years to come.
Ye may shout, ye fourscore million strong,
　　For the mills that spin and the fields that thrive;
Give feast, and frolic, and speech and song,
　　And guns for the Union forty and five;
But ring sweet bells for the souls unseen
Who fought your fight in the Old Thirteen.

On the sky-born flag of your Mother States,
　　Bright with their own and their children's stars,
The herald finger of Fame relates
　　Their story in crimson saber-scars;
And northern winter and southern heat
　　Shall ebb and flow to their silken swell
O'er the domes where civic sages meet
　　And the roofs where striplings read and spell,
Till the youngest learn what its colors mean,
And honor the stripes of the Old Thirteen.

In the splendor of Independence morn
  Flame high the banner from East to West,
And summon with Freedom's bugle-horn
  The brood of your eagle's farthest nest;
But dress the fallows where childhood grows
  Untried to the Century just begun,
Till the hands of the Union clasp and close
  Round greener laurels of Washington,
And schoolboys harvest the years between
The seed and the fruit of the Old Thirteen.

  * * * * * * *

New Knights of a new age! rally your band
  To the fields of Peace with trowel and spade,
Till the bounds of your schoolhouse realm are spanned
  With beds of beauty and bowers of shade.
For the souls of Adams and Gadsden speak,
  From the Liberty Tree of Boston Bay,
From the Liberty Tree of Sugar Creek,
  And you hear their breeze-borne voices say,
"Young patriots, keep your garden green
That was bought with the blood of the Old Thirteen!

"Every shrub you plant by the scholar's path
  Stands sentinel to your free estate,
And shame to riot and wrong and wrath
  Is the lily at Learning's nursery gate!"
And the spirits of Hancock and Brevard
  From the strife and glory of long ago
Will proudly visit each blooming yard
  And breathe its breath in the summer glow
Where the hovering elm and live-oak lean
O'er the playmate race of the Old Thirteen.

By permission of *The Youth's Companion.*

THE RED, WHITE AND BLUE

D. T. SHAW.

1. O Co - lum - bia, the gem   of the o - cean,   The   home   of the
2. When   war wing'd its wide des - o - la - tion,   And   threat - en'd the
3. The   star - span-gled ban - ner bring hith - er,   O'er Co - lum - bia's true

brave and the   free,   The shrine   of each pa - triot's de - vo - tion,
land   to de - form,   The ark   then of free - dom's foun - da - tion,
sons let   it   wave; May the wreaths they have won   nev - er   with - er,

A   world of - fers hom - age   to thee!   Thy   man - dates make
Co -   lum - bia rode safe thro' the storm: With the gar - lands of
Nor its   stars cease to shine on the brave.   May the serv - ice u -

he - roes as - sem - ble,   When   Lib - er - ty's   form stands in view;
vic - t'ry a - round her,   When so proud - ly she   bore her brave crew,
ni - ted ne'er sev - er,   But   hold   to their col - ors so true;

By permission of Ginn Publishing Co.

THE RED, WHITE AND BLUE—Concluded

Thy ban - ners make tyr - an - ny trem - ble, When borne by the
With her flag proud - ly float - ing be - fore her The boast of the
The ar - my and na - vy for - ev - er! Three cheers for the

red, white and blue, When borne by the red, white and blue, When
red, white and blue, The boast of the red, white and blue, The
red, white and blue, Three cheers for the red, white and blue, Three

borne by the red, white and blue, Thy ban - ners make
boast of the red, white and blue, With her flag proud - ly
cheers for the red, white and blue, The ar - my and

tyr - an - ny trem - ble, When borne by the red, white and blue.
float - ing be - fore her, The boast of the red, white and blue.
na - vy for - ev - er! Three cheers for the red, white and blue!

HAIL TO OUR FLAG

Speed our republic, O Father on high!
  Lead us in pathways of justice and right;
Rulers as well as the ruled, one and all,
  Girdle of virtue—the armor of might!
Hail! three times hail to our country and flag!

Foremost in battle for Freedom to stand,
  We rush to arms when roused by its call;
Still as of yore when George Washington led,
  Thunders our war cry, We conquer or fall!
Hail! three times hail to our country and flag!

Rise up, proud eagle, rise up to the clouds,
  Spread thy broad wings o'er this fair western world!
Fling from thy beak our dear banner of old!
  Show that it still is for Freedom unfurled!
Hail! three times hail to our country and flag!

A HOLY STANDARD

F. MARION CRAWFORD

In radiance heavenly fair,
Floats on the peaceful air
  That flag that never stooped from victory's pride;
Those stars that softly gleam,
Those stripes that o'er us stream,
  In war's grand agony were sanctified;
A holy standard, pure and free,
To light the home of peace, or blaze in victory.

"The Flag to the Right Ever True"

127

ROLL CALL

NATHANIEL GRAHAM SHEPHERD

"Corporal Green!" the orderly cried.
  "Here!" was the answer, loud and clear,
  From the lips of the soldier who stood near;
And "Here!" was the word the next replied.

"Cyrus Drew!"—then silence fell,
  This time no answer followed the call;
  Only his rear man had seen him fall,
Killed or wounded, he could not tell.

There they stood in the failing light,
  These men of battle, with grave, dark looks,
  As plain to be read as open books,
While slowly gathered the shades of night.

The fern on the hill-side was splashed with blood,
  And down in the corn, where the poppies grew,
  Were redder stains than the poppies knew,
And crimson-dyed was the river's flood.

For the foe had crossed from the other side
  That day, in face of a murderous fire
  That swept them down in its terrible ire,
And their life-blood went to color the tide.

"Herbert Kline!" At the call there came
  Two stalwart soldiers into the line,
  Bearing between them this Herbert Kline,
Wounded and bleeding, to answer his name.

"Ezra Kerr!"—and a voice answered "Here!"
  "Hiram Kerr!" but no man replied.
  They were brothers, these two; the sad wind sighed,
And a shudder crept through the cornfield near.

"Ephraim Deane!"—then a soldier spoke:
  "Deane carried our regiment's colors," he said;
  "Where our ensign was shot I left him dead,
Just after the enemy wavered and broke.

"Close to the roadside his body lies;
  I paused a moment and gave him drink;
  He murmured his mother's name, I think,
And death came with it and closed his eyes."

'Twas a victory, yes, but it cost us dear;
  For that company's roll, when called at night,
  Of a hundred men who went into the fight,
Numbered but twenty that answered "Here!"

CROSSING THE RAPPAHANNOCK

ANONYMOUS

They leaped in the rocking shallops—
  Ten offered where one could go—
And the breeze was alive with laughter,
  Till the boatmen began to row.

Then the shore, where the rebels harbored,
  Was fringed with a gush of flame,
And buzzing like bees o'er the water
  The swarms of their bullets came.

In silence how dread and solemn,
  With courage how grand and true,
Steadily, steadily onward
  The line of the shallops drew.

Not a whisper! Each man was conscious
  He stood in the sight of death,
So he bowed to the awful presence
  And treasured his living breath.

'Twixt death in the air above them,
  And death in the waves below,
Through ball and grape and shrapnel
  They moved—my God, how slow!

And many a brave, stout fellow,
  Who sprang in the boats with mirth,
Ere they made that fatal crossing
  Was a load of lifeless earth.

And many a brave, stout fellow,
  Whose limbs with strength were rife,
Was torn and crushed and shattered—
  A helpless wreck for life.

But yet the boats moved onward;
  Through fire and lead they drove,
With the dark, still mass within them,
  And the floating stars above.

They formed in line of battle—
  Not a man was out of place;
Then with leveled steel they hurled them
  Straight in the rebels' face.

THE MEANING OF OUR FLAG

HENRY WARD BEECHER

If one asks me the meaning of our flag, I say to him: It means just what Concord and Lexington meant, what Bunker Hill meant. It means the whole glorious Revolutionary War. It means all that the Declaration of Independence meant. It means all that the Constitution of our people, organizing for justice, for liberty, and for happiness, meant.

Under this banner rode Washington and his armies. Before it Burgoyne laid down his arms. It waved on the highlands at West

Point. When Arnold would have surrendered these valuable fortresses and precious legacies, his day was turned into night and his treachery was driven away by the beams of light from his starry banner.

It cheered our army, driven out from around New York, and in their painful pilgrimages through New Jersey. This banner streamed in light over the soldiers' heads at Valley Forge and at Morristown. It crossed the waters rolling with ice at Trenton, and when its stars gleamed in the cold morning with victory, a new day dawned on the despondency of this nation.

Our flag carries American ideas, American history, and American feelings. Beginning with the colonies, and coming down to our time, in its sacred heraldry, in its glorious insignia, it has gathered and stored chiefly this supreme idea: divine right of liberty in man. Every color means liberty; every thread means liberty; every form of star and beam or stripe of light means liberty—not lawlessness, not license, but organized, institutional liberty—liberty through law, and laws for liberty!

This American Flag was the safeguard of liberty. Not an atom of crown was allowed to go into its insignia. Not a symbol of authority in the ruler was permitted to go into it. It was an ordinance of liberty by the people, for the people. That it meant, that it means, and, by the blessing of God, that it shall mean to the end of time!

9—*The Story of the American Flag.*

BATTLE HYMN OF THE REPUBLIC

MRS. JULIA WARD HOWE

President Theodore Roosevelt's favorite poem, suggested by him for this volume.

Mine eyes have seen the glory of the coming of the Lord;
He is trampling out the vintage where the grapes of wrath are stored;
He hath loosed the fateful lightnings of his terrible swift sword.
His truth is marching on.

CHORUS.

Glory! Glory! Hallelujah!
Glory! Glory! Hallelujah!
Glory! Glory! Hallelujah!
His truth is marching on.

I have seen Him in the watchfires of an hundred circling camps;
They have builded Him an altar 'mid the evening dews and damps,
I can read His righteous sentence by the dim and flaring lamps;
His day is marching on.

I have read His fiery gospel writ in rows of burnished steel:
"As ye deal with my contemners, so with you my grace shall deal."
Let the hero, born of woman, crush the serpent with his heel;
Since God is marching on.

He has sounded forth a trumpet that shall never call "retreat."
He is searching out the hearts of men before His judgment seat,
Be swift my soul to answer Him; be jubilant my feet;
Our God is marching on.

In the beauty of the lilies Christ was born across the sea,
With a beauty in His bosom that transfigures you and me.
As He died to make men holy, let us die to make men free,
While God is marching on.

The Spirit of '76

A SONG FOR OUR FLAG

MARGARET E. SANGSTER

A bit of color against the blue:
Hues of the morning, blue for true,
And red for the kindling light of flame,
And white for a nation's stainless fame.
Oh! fling it forth to the winds afar,
With hope in its every shining star;
Under its folds wherever found,
Thank God, we have freedom's holy ground.

Don't you love it, as out it floats
From the school house peak, and glad young throats
Sing of the banner that aye shall be
Symbol of honor and victory?

Don't you thrill when the marching feet
Of jubilant soldiers shake the street,
And the bugles shrill, and the trumpets call,
And the red, white, and blue is over us all?
Don't you pray, amid starting tears,
It may never be furled through age-long years?

A song for our flag, our country's boast,
That gathers beneath it a mighty host;
Long may it wave o'er the goodly land
We hold in fee 'neath our Father's hand.
For God and liberty evermore
May that banner stand from shore to shore,
Never to those high meanings lost,
Never with alien standards crossed,
But always valiant and pure and true,
Our starry flag: red, white and blue.

WASHINGTON RAISING THE FLAG ON FORT DUQUESNE

135

THE MAN WHO WEARS THE BUTTON

BY JOHN MELLEN THURSTON, SENATOR FROM NEBRASKA

Sometimes in passing along the street I meet a man who, in the left lapel of his coat, wears a little, plain, modest, unassuming bronze button. The coat is often old and rusty; the face above it seamed and furrowed by the toil and suffering of adverse years; perhaps beside it hangs an empty sleeve, and below it stumps a wooden peg. But when I meet the man who wears that button I doff my hat and stand uncovered in his presence—yea! to me the very dust his weary foot has pressed is holy ground, for I know that man, in the dark hours of the nation's peril, bared his breast to the hell of battle to keep the flag of our country in the Union sky.

Maybe at Donaldson he reached the inner trench; at Shiloh held the broken line; at Chattanooga climbed the flame-swept hill, or stormed the clouds on Lookout Heights. He was not born or bred to soldier life. His country's summons called him from the plow, the forge, the bench, the loom, the mine, the store, the office, the college, the sanctuary. He did not fight for greed of gold, to find adventure, or to win renown. He loved the peace of quiet ways, and yet he broke the clasp of clinging arms, turned from the witching glance of tender eyes, left good-by kisses upon tiny lips to look death in the face on desperate fields.

And when the war was over he quietly took up the broken threads of love and life as best he could, a better citizen for having been so good a soldier.

What mighty men have worn this same bronze button! Grant, Sherman, Sheridan, Logan, and an hundred more, whose names are written on the title-page of deathless fame. Their glorious victories are known of men; the history of their country gives them voice; the white light of publicity illuminates them for every eye. But there are thousands who, in humbler way, no less deserve applause. How many knightliest acts of chivalry were never seen beyond the line or heard of above the roar of battle.

God bless the men who wore the button! They pinned the stars of Union in the azure of our flag with bayonets, and made atonement for a nation's sin in blood. They took the negro from the auction-block and at the altar of emancipation crowned him—citizen. They supplemented "Yankee Doodle" with "Glory Hallelujah," and Yorktown with Appomatox. Their powder woke the morn of universal freedom and made the name "American" first in all the earth. To us their memory is an inspiration and to the future it is hope.

"MANY IN ONE"

FROM "OUR HOLIDAYS," ARRANGED BY MATILDA BLAIR

The last bell rings, and in they pour,
Like nations through our country's door.
Stand here and watch them as they pass,
While I present to you the class.
These days our methods are so ripe
We teachers learn to know the type:
First comes young Patrick bright and keen,
Whose father came from the Island Green.
Next, Gretchen, with her flaxen hair,
And quaintly stolid German air.
Small Levi, who will not disdain
The crudest bargain, fraught with gain.
Antonio, whose dusky eyes
Seem ardent as Italian skies.
Petite Corinne, with piquant face,
Fair France in her unconscious grace.
Yet from each eye, gray, dark, or blue,
A patriot's soul looks out at you.
And mark how true their voices ring
When of the Stars and Stripes they sing!
Oh! whisper not of race or clan
To our staunch young American.
That flag above us in the sun
Has merged the Many into One.

By permission of McLoughlin Brothers.

THE BLUE AND THE GRAY

*In 1869 the women of Columbus, Miss., * * *   strewed flowers alike on the graves of the Confederate and of the Union soldiers.*

FRANCIS MILES FINCH

By the flow of the inland river,
Whence the fleets of iron have fled,
Where the blades of the grave-grass quiver,
Asleep are the ranks of the dead,—
Under the sod and the dew,
Waiting the judgment-day:
Under the one, the Blue;
Under the other, the Gray.

These, in the robings of glory;
Those, in the gloom of defeat;
All, with the battle-blood gory,
In the dusk of eternity meet,—
Under the sod and the dew,
Waiting the judgment-day:
Under the laurel, the Blue;
Under the willow, the Gray.

From the silence of sorrowful hours,
The desolate mourners go,
Lovingly laden with flowers,
Alike for the friend and the foe,—
Under the sod and the dew,
Waiting the judgment-day:
Under the roses, the Blue;
Under the lilies, the Gray.

So with an equal splendor,
The morning sun-rays fall,
With a touch impartially tender,
On the blossoms blooming for all,—
Under the sod and the dew,
Waiting the judgment-day:
Broidered with gold, the Blue;
Mellowed with gold, the Gray.

So when the summer calleth,
On forest and field of grain,
With an equal murmur falleth,
The cooling drip of the rain,—
Under the sod and the dew,
Waiting the judgment-day:
Wet with the rain, the Blue;
Wet with the rain, the Gray.

Sadly, but not with upbraiding,
The generous deed was done;
In the gloom of years that are fading,
No braver battle was won,—
Under the sod and the dew,
Waiting the judgment-day:
Under the blossoms, the Blue;
Under the garlands, the Gray.

No more shall the war-cry sever,
Or the winding rivers be red;
They banish our anger forever,
When they laurel the graves of our dead,—
Under the sod and the dew,
Waiting the judgment-day:
Love and tears, for the Blue;
Tears and love, for the Gray.

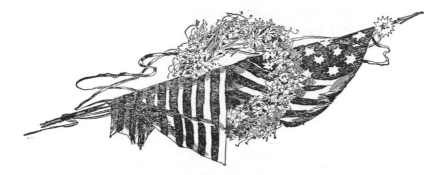

SPECIAL DAYS TO FLY THE FLAG

January 1.   New Year's Day. Lincoln's Emancipation Proclamation.........1863
February 12. Lincoln's Birthday 1809
February 22. Washington's Birthday 1732
February 27. Longfellow's Birthday 1807
March 4.   First United States Congress.................................1789
              Inauguaration of President (once every four years).
March 17.   British Evacuated Boston (St. Patrick's Day)....................1776
April   Arbor Day. Date varies in different States.
April 19.   Patriots' Day. Battles of Lexington and Concord................1775
May 4.   Birthday of Horace Mann......................................1796
May 18.   Peace Day, First Meeting of The Hague Arbitration Court........1899
May 30.   Memorial or Decoration Day.
June 14.   Flag Day. Stars and Stripes adopted by Congress..............1777
June 17.   Battle of Bunker Hill..1775
July 4.   Independence Day. Declaration of Independence................1776
September   (First Monday) Labor Day.
September 10. Perry's Victory on Lake Erie.................................1813
September 13. Bombardment of Fort McHenry, during which Francis Scott Key
              wrote "The Star Spangled Banner" 1814
September 17. Constitution Adopted 1789
October 12.   Columbus Discovered America.................................1492
October 19.   Surrender of Cornwallis......................................1781
November   (First Tuesday Election Day).
November   (Last Thursday) Thanksgiving Day.
December 17. Birthday of Whittier...1807
December 21. Forefathers' Day. The Landing of the Pilgrims................1620

FLAG PHRASES

To "hoist" or "raise a flag," is to draw the banner to the top of a pole, staff or mast, usually for the first time, as Washington did, at Cambridge, Massachusetts, January 1, 1776, and Lincoln raised a new flag over Independence Hall, Philadelphia, February 22, 1861.

To "dip the flag" is to lower it slightly then raise it quickly, as on shipboard, to salute another vessel or a fort.

The "flag at half-mast" means mourning. When a President, Governor, or other high official dies, flags are lowered half way, or "at half-mast," as a sign of mourning. Sometimes the memory of a private citizen, not an official, is honored in this way. Fishing craft and other vessels returning with flags at half-mast show that some one has been lost at sea.

To "strike the flag" is to lower it altogether as a sign of surrender or submission.

A "flag of truce" is a white flag to show a desire for conference or parley.

The "white flag" may be a sign of peace. It is often displayed by either or both sides after a battle, to allow surgeons, nurses, and others to care for the wounded and bury the dead.

The "Red-Cross flag" is the banner of the great, humane Red-Cross Society respected by all civilized nations. Physicans, surgeons, nurses, of this society go wherever they are needed, with ambulances, hospitals, etc., for those suffering in war, plagues and so on.

The "yellow flag" is a sign of quarantine, a signal of warning that beneath it is a dangerous disease which is "catching," or contagious. It was first used only as a yellow fever signal.

The "red flag" was first used as an auction sign, then as a danger signal. It is now a sign of defiance and is the flag of anarchists or people who do not believe in government, and threaten to break up society.

The "black flag" used to be the flag of pirates, or sea robbers. With the skull and cross-bones it meant death to all on board the captured vessel, or "no quarter"—which meant no mercy would be shown to man, woman or child.

FROM "JOHN BURNS OF GETTYSBURG"

BY BRET HARTE

Just where the tide of battle turns,
Erect and lonely, stood old John Burns.
How do you think the old man was dressed?
He wore an ancient, long buff vest,
Yellow as saffron—but his best;
And, buttoned over his manly breast,
Was a bright blue coat with a rolling collar,
And large gilt buttons—size of a dollar—
With tails that country folk called "swaller."
He wore a broad-brimmed, bell-crowned hat,
White as the locks on which it sat.
Never had such a sight been seen
For forty years on the village green,
Since old John Burns was a country beau,
And went to the "quiltings" long ago.

Close at his elbow all that day,
Veterans of the Peninsula,
Sunburnt and bearded, charged away;
And striplings, downy of lip and chin—

Clerks that the Home Guard mustered in—
Glanced, as they passed, at the hat he wore,
Then at the rifle his right hand bore;
And hailed him, from out their youthful lore,
With scraps of a slangy repertoire:
"How are you, White Hat?" "Put her through!"
"Your head's level!" and "Bully for you!"
Called him "Daddy"—begged he'd disclose
The name of the tailor who made his clothes,
And what was the value he set on those;
While Burns, unmindful of jeer or scoff,
Stood there picking the rebels off—
With his long brown rifle, and bell-crowned hat,
And the swallow tails they were laughing at.

It was but a moment, for that respect
Which clothes all courage their voices checked;
And something the wildest could understand
Spake in the old man's strong right hand,
And his corded throat, and the lurking frown
Of his eyebrows under his old bell-crown;
Until, as they gazed, there crept an awe
Through the ranks in whispers, and some men saw,
In the antique vestments and long white hair,
The Past of the Nation in battle there;
And some of the soldiers since declare
That the gleam of his old white hat afar,
Like the crested plume of the brave Navarre,
That day was their oriflamme of war.

So raged the battle. You know the rest:
How the rebels, beaten and backward pressed,
Broke at the final charge and ran.
At which John Burns—a practical man —
Shouldered his rifle, unbent his brows,
And then went back to his bees and cows.

A SUMMARY OF SOME FLAG FACTS

In 1606, in honor of the union of England and Scotland, the English flag, which for years had been white with the red cross of St. George extending to its edges was changed to a field of blue, across which was placed the upright red cross of St. George and the diagonal white cross of St. Andrew.

This was the flag that floated over the "Susan Constant" at James-town and the "Mayflower" at Plymouth. Although the colonies frequently used devices of their own, the English flag was the flag of this country for more than one hundred and fifty years.

So different were the symbols of the colonies, regiments and ships that Washington, in 1775, wrote, "Please fix on some flag by which our vessels may know each other."

The first striped flag was raised at Washington's headquarters, Cambridge, Massachusetts, January 2nd, 1776, and saluted with thirteen guns. About the same time John Paul Jones, as senior First Lieutenant, hoisted it with his own hands over Commodore Hopkins' flagship the "Alfred," then lying in the Delaware at Philadelphia.

In 1777 Congress appointed a committee consisting of General Washington, Robert Morris and Colonel Ross "to designate a suitable flag for the nation." This committee, as all the world knows, conferred with Mistress Betsy Ross, and afterward recommended a flag in which the stripes recently introduced were retained, but in which the crosses, the symbol of British authority, gave place to the stars which were henceforth to shine for liberty.

On June 14th, 1777, in old Independence Hall, Philadelphia, Congress adopted the following resolution: "Resolved, that the flag of the thirteen United States be thirteen stripes, alternate red and white; that the union be thirteen stars, white in a blue field, representing a new constellation. The stars to be arranged in a circle." Enter here the Star Spangled Banner, with thirty-seven years to wait for the song that was to immortalize the name.

The Stars and Stripes was first used in actual military service at Fort Stanwix, re-named Fort Schuyler, now Rome, N. Y., on August 6th, 1777, and first carried in battle at a skirmish at Cooch's Bridge, near Wilmington, Delaware, September 3rd, 1777.

On February 14th, 1778, Captain John Paul Jones had the great satisfaction of seeing the Stars and Stripes "recognized for the first time and in the fullest manner by the flag of France" by salutes first to the "Ranger" and later to the "Independence" of Jones' fleet. This was probably the first recognition by any foreign power of the colors of the United States of America.

John Paul Jones was also the first to see a regular British Man-of-War strike her flag to that of the United States. Jones received his appointment to the command of the "Ranger" on the very day that our national flag was adopted by Congress. He said "That flag and I are twins. We cannot be parted in life or in death. So long as we can float, we shall float together; if we must sink, we shall go down as one."

The flag was not changed until 1795, when two stripes and two stars were added for Vermont and Kentucky. By 1816 four more states, Tennessee, Ohio, Louisiana and Indiana were in the family and a committee was appointed to give them a place on the flag. Realizing that there must be a limit to the stripes, the committee made a recommendation which was adopted April 4th, 1818, that the flag be permanently thirteen stripes, representing the original thirteen states and that a new star be added for each state as admitted.

The plan of arranging the stars to form one large star was abandoned at that time and the method of placing them in rows was adopted. Since then a star had been added to the flag on the Fourth of July following the admission of a state to the Union.

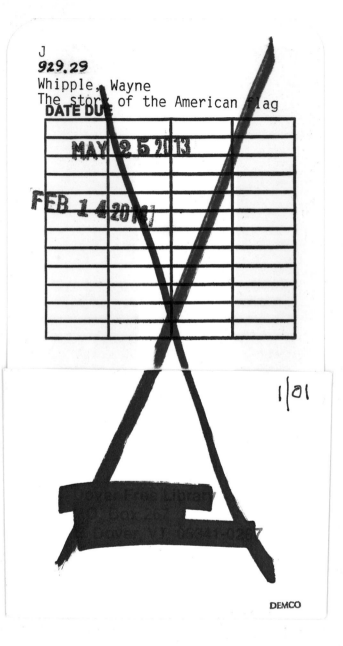